The Talent Pool

The Talent Pool

How to Find and Keep
Dedicated People
While Making a Lasting Impact

SHARON RYAN
CYNTHIA TOLSMA

EXPERT PRESS

The Talent Pool
How to Find and Keep Dedicated People
While Making a Lasting Impact

© 2019 Sharon Ryan & Cynthia Tolsma

ISBN-13: 978-1-946203-52-6

Dasher, Inc.
777 East Park Drive
Harrisburg, PA 17111
717-234-3274
www.dasherinc.com

www.ExpertPress.net

Contents

Acknowledgments

Many individuals participated in and supported the continuing development of this book and the comprehensive support system Dasher developed for low-wage, economically fragile workers.

The authors greatly appreciate and acknowledge Tracey Glenn, Dasher's president; Edward Dame, Dasher's chief operating officer; and Bonnie Meisel, Dasher's chief financial officer, for their contributions to the development of all aspects of the Dasher *Team Member Prosperity and Success Model.*

We are also grateful for Regina Vercilla, Jewel Cooper, and Ellen Smith, MD, who offered valuable insights, comments, and guidance on how to strengthen the Dasher *Team Member Prosperity and Success Model* and the explanations that we provided.

Many leaders and authors have influenced and inspired us. We thank John Dame, Teresa Miller, Dave Ramsey, Seth Godin, David Friedman, Tom Foster, Leila Janah, Gino Wickman, and Carol Dweck. Judith Jones and Michael DeLon played important roles in all aspects of drafting and publishing this book. We also are grateful for the stellar business guidance provided by Vistage International and the Entrepreneurial Operating System (EOS).

Finally, we are sincerely grateful for our Dasher Team and their very impressive contributions to the success of Dasher and to the fulfillment of Dasher's purpose to help people lead happy, healthy lives. As we often say to each other, Dasher is not an *it*. Dasher is *us*. That means each of you is making impressive strides in your own right and living the Dasher Way. It is an honor to share the journey with all of you.

Sharon Ryan
Cynthia Tolsma

Introduction

AT DASHER, WE BELIEVE that every human being is of equal value and that everyone deserves to be heard. We are committed to creating equal access to prosperity as each of us defines it for ourselves. What's more, we know that creating a company culture based on these principles leads to economic success for both Dasher and our people.

Dasher exists to help people live happy, healthy lives. That's our mission, not only for our clients but also for our employees. Dasher is an example of a successful for-profit business that is committed to supporting economically fragile people. That may sound counterintuitive—we often get asked if we are a nonprofit organization—but we are a business, and a thriving one. In fact, we believe our way of doing business is what makes us successful.

Dasher's workforce includes many low-wage, economically fragile people. Ten years ago, we concluded that paying higher wages and offering comprehensive benefits to low-wage, economically fragile employees did not measurably improve employee retention or drastically improve quality of life.

After searching in vain for a proven system that employers can use for helping low-wage, economically fragile workers to live happy, healthy lives, the Dasher Management Team developed its own *Team Member Prosperity and Success Model,* an innovative business process that portrays an end-to-end solution.

The Talent Pool explains in detail our comprehensive plan—with measurable results—that was developed through trial and error by a talented, committed group of social entrepreneurs. Dasher's *Team Member Prosperity and Success Model* is a blueprint for providing individual and group support, leadership, personal development, and professional development specifically for low-wage economically fragile workers. This model reduces turnover, increases productivity, and puts economically fragile workers on the path to economic stability.

For employers, there is a clear economic benefit that arises from caring more about the quality of life experienced by economically fragile workers. It comes from maximizing returns on employee recruitment, reducing the cost of employee turnover, and differentiating the business in the eyes of customers and prospects as both a socially responsible and an economically successful partner.

Why should you read this book?

If you are operating a business, you need to understand that economically fragile people are vital to the success of your business, whether they are employees, customers, or constituents. Economically fragile people are young and old, from every race, creed, and gender. Economically fragile people are talented and dedicated, and they are great teammates. Economically fragile people are uncertain about the continuous availability of life's basic necessities for themselves and other people for whom they are responsible. Economically fragile people are typically low-wage earners with numerous obstacles and limited opportunities to become economically stable.

The U.S. Department of Labor Bureau of Labor Statistics is a rich source of data that supports key points about our workforce.

According to this source, in the fourth quarter of 2018, the median usual weekly earnings of service professionals working full time was $574.00.[1]

That translates into approximately $27,500 annually, or somewhere in the range of $13.00 per hour. While we explain that income is not the sole indicator of who is economically fragile, it is certainly a factor, and many people in the United States are affected by issues we discuss in this book.

We are experts at influencing people who are economically fragile. This book describes what we have learned about how to recruit, engage, support, and retain employees who are economically fragile.

There are at least four good reasons to read this book: (1) Business expansion is dependent on employee retention, and business growth is often constrained by a lack of available labor, which makes tapping into the talent pool of economically fragile people imperative; (2) Efforts to influence economically fragile people repeatedly fail due to the lack of understanding of this population; (3) Brand connection with consumers is strengthened when that brand is actively making a difference in the world; and (4) Helping low-wage economically fragile employees to become economically stable creates a competitive advantage.

Business Expansion

Workforce expansion is a bottleneck for business expansion in markets with few available workers. Enabling economically fragile people to become successful employees expands the workforce and provides a rich source of talent and innovation. People naturally want to work, to contribute to a meaningful goal, and to be the masters of their own destiny. Low-wage, economically fragile people are no exception.

The U.S. Department of Labor Bureau of Labor Statistics reported, in January 2019, that US businesses hired at a rate of 3.9 percent and lost workers at a combined rate of 7.1 percent.[2]

Service continuity and institutional knowledge are being decimated. As one astute business professional noted, "this rate of employee turnover is a death blow." We see it as a ripe opportunity for businesses that seek to embrace the concepts we incorporate into Dasher's *Team Member Prosperity and Success Model.*

Tapping into the talent pool of economically fragile workers presents some special challenges, risks, and rewards. Traditional workforce management approaches used today are failing as evidenced by double- and triple-digit employee turnover rates.

This infographic produced by the Society of Human Resource Management (SHRM) adds more useful data .

(Reproduced with permission)

To offset high turnover, many employers are innovating to improve their processes for recruiting new employees. In our experience, operating a business where employees want to stay makes recruiting much easier, increases agility, and makes the business more profitable.

We have the results to prove it. Dasher is an example of a successful, for-profit business carefully and consciously developed to get a return on its investment of time and money to attract and engage with a workforce comprised largely of low-wage, economically fragile workers.

Employee retention is a key driver of business expansion. It saves money, increases productivity, and drives the ability to create a strong culture. Culture is a key aspect of the Dasher *Team Member Prosperity and Success Model*.

We explain this in detail in Chapters 4-9, describing each step in the model.

Influence

In our experience, low-wage, economically fragile people are very aware of the precarious existence that they have and mostly consider it undignified. From our standpoint, the opposite of poverty is not wealth, it is dignity. That is why the idea of maintaining the individual's dignity and pride flows through everything that we do.

Typical approaches to influencing the behavior of economically fragile people often fail to respect their inherent dignity. Such approaches may include offering financial handouts that are humiliating, implementing would-be incentive programs that do not incentivize, or meddling in people's lives with no invitation.

The Dasher *Team Member Prosperity and Success Model* influences behavior using respectful, dignified communication and by providing techniques specially designed for use with low-wage, economically fragile people.

Economically fragile people are justifiably proud of the extreme effort they devote to carving out a life under difficult circumstances. They want to be engaged in the pursuit of meaningful goals and feel part of something that is bigger than they are. They seek—and they deserve—to live a life without unwanted outside interference. We describe the characteristics of economically fragile people in Chapter 1.

Brand Loyalty

A study completed by the Marketing Science Institute (MSI) concluded that brand preference allowed consumer product companies to charge an average of a 26 percent premium on their prices. The study shows a variety of positive impacts of brand on cash flow, profits, and firm value.

For a summary, see "The Financial Power of Brand Preference," published in January 2019 in *Forbes Magazine* online.[3]

Consumer research makes it clear that businesses must have a positive social impact to earn positive brand loyalty. A white paper published by Deloitte in 2015 titled "Driving corporate growth through social Impact: Four corporate archetypes to maximize your social impact," describes five ways that social impact creates value for businesses. The Deloitte white paper reports that 53 percent of Fortune 500 companies are focused on strengthening relationships with purchasers by engaging in activities that have a social impact.[4]

Vague claims about saving the environment are being replaced with specific, measurable social contributions. Dasher's *Team Member Prosperity and Success Model* works well in an environment in which the basis for consumer opinion is shifting and converging into a combination of business and philanthropy.

Business leaders know that the people to whom they are selling their products or services often will not take the time to understand the subtle differences that make a product or a service better. Combining a business model with caring about quality of life for economically fragile people can produce a clear economic benefit and differentiate a business as both socially responsible and economically successful. We discuss this more in Chapter 11, The Dasher Challenge.

Competitive Advantage

We base much of our success in business on the theory that it is better to be different than it is to be better. What makes Dasher different is a deeply-rooted, measurable commitment to creating economic prosperity for all people.

And here is the real competitive advantage: People want to join our team. Talented people seek us out. Customers want to do business with us. They want to partner with us. Our clients expect phenomenal execution; that is a given. They are also saying, "We really love the fact that by hiring you and paying you, we are supporting this revolutionary good work that you are doing."

As we began developing the *Team Member Prosperity and Success Model*, we looked more closely at how to identify the characteristics of low-wage, economically fragile workers. As we learned how to eliminate stereotypes from our thought process, we realized just how vastly uninformed we were about who is economically fragile and why. We discuss what we have learned in the next chapter.

Chapter 1

Who Are the Economically Fragile?

Economically fragile people are uncertain about the continuous availability of life's basic necessities for themselves and other people for whom they are responsible. Economically fragile people routinely experience financial insecurity, food insecurity, housing insecurity, and transportation insecurity. All of these are explained in more detail in this chapter.

As an employer, you may be wondering whether you have any economically fragile workers. Or you may be wondering how you can stop the double- or triple-digit turnover occurring in your low-wage workforce.

Organizations seeking to influence low-wage, economically fragile people are often surprised to find them elusive and non-responsive to offers of assistance and fringe benefits. The organization making the offer may consider acceptance to be a no-brainer, but that decision may not be so simple.

From personal experience, we know that economically fragile people do their very best to make everyone think that they do not have any problems at all when they do, in fact, have serious problems.

Why do people go to great lengths to conceal their economic fragility? To maintain their dignity. The undignified aspects of being economically fragile—not being able to cover costs for basic needs—motivate proud people to fly under our radar. This is why trust is a key element in supporting and influencing low-wage, economically fragile workers. We focus more on this in our discussion of culture.

Why not swallow pride and accept offers of what will make life better? The degree of complexity (not to mention the degree of stress) in the lives of people who are economically fragile is mind-blowing. Tunnel vision occurs naturally, and the pressure erodes decision-making skills.

Why would someone leave a job for five cents more an hour? Low-wage, economically fragile workers change jobs because another five cents an hour is another hundred dollars closer to becoming financially stable.

Very slowly, employers are increasing worker pay, benefits, and hours to maximize returns on employee recruitment and reduce the cost of employee turnover. Even though projected savings from lower turnover make paying slightly higher wages justifiable in a spreadsheet, market trends show this does not really impact turnover that much.

The *Team Member Prosperity and Success Model* developed by Dasher breaks the cycle of recurring turnover. Our experience shows that low-wage workers are more likely to forgo an extra five cents per hour when they are immersed in a carefully created, relentlessly curated, supportive culture that preserves dignity, cultivates trust, and provides a pathway to financial security.

Recognizing the Signs of Economic Fragility

Early on in our process development, we focused on identifying economically fragile people who wanted to remain undetected. We never went directly to our teammates. We never implied, asked, or inferred anything. We learned that this is an ongoing process that requires some counterintuitive thinking and powers of observation.

As a starting point, some businesses may want to understand the potential scope of the issue from a high-level perspective. The U.S. Census Bureau offers easy access to demographic data that can help businesses begin to quantify economically fragile employees in the workforce. Data shows that median household income is generally higher in urban counties; poverty rates tend to be higher in rural counties.[5]

A more detailed demographic breakdown can be found in the Census Bureau's 2013-2017 American Community Survey (ACS) five-year estimates, released in December 2018. The ACS includes more than 40 social, economic, housing, and demographic topics, including homeownership rates and costs, health insurance, and educational attainment, broken down for each of the nation's 3,142 counties.[6]

County-level geography profiles are available in a visual format with maps, charts, and graphs. These profiles cover a variety of topics including income, commuting, homeownership, and veterans, incorporating not only the ACS but also business and industry data from the 2012 Economic Census, 2016 County Business Patterns, and 2012 Survey of Business Owners.[7]

The Census Bureau's Survey of Income and Program Participation (SIPP) collects information on the short-term dynamics of employment, income, household composition, and eligibility and participation in government assistance programs. This nationally representative panel survey is a valuable source of information on such topics as economic well-being, family dynamics, education, wealth and assets, health insurance, child care, and food security.[8]

Having this data is helpful for defining potential issues, though it is inconclusive. This may be surprising. Gross income is not a good indicator of whether a person is economically fragile. Some low-wage workers may have safety nets, places to go, resources accumulated, and deep backup plans. People with moderate to high salaries may have mortgage-sized payments for their student loans, no safety net, and episodes of periodic financial insecurity which can lead to chronic financial insecurity.

How can you recognize economic fragility among your employees? As a first cut, ask this simple question: Who has attendance issues?

Of course, this is not an instant qualifier or instant disqualifier, but frequent absence may be one of the first signs of economic fragility. Why? There are many reasons. Economic fragility can lead people to being absent from work and to being unhealthy. They may be absent because they are not sleeping, because they have issues with transportation or childcare, because they are sick from stress, or because somebody else in their life is sick.

The key to recognizing the signs of economic fragility is simply to look for them. If you look carefully, they are not that difficult to see. The following are some additional indicators of economic fragility.

When a low-wage worker is the only working person in a multi-person household, there is a good chance they may be economically fragile. Rarely can a family relying upon a single low-wage earner be financially secure. For example, in Dauphin County, Pennsylvania, the hourly rate that an individual full-time worker must earn to support a three-person household is $29.11/hour.[9]

People driving an older model car with unrepaired body damage may be economically fragile. The cost to repair a vehicle that is not insured for physical damage is beyond the means of people struggling to survive. Food, clothing, shelter, and medical care leave nothing extra for unplanned expenses.

Relying on the emergency room when they or their family are ill may mean that a person is economically fragile. They cannot see a physician without losing work hours so they will seek care for themselves and family members in off hours.

A low-wage earner with a spouse or children who have been involved with the legal system may be economically fragile. This is not only because the cost of helping with a legal situation creates a financial crisis, but also because anyone caught up in the legal system will find that a criminal record makes it difficult or impossible to find sustained employment that would contribute to the household's financial stability.

Sometimes the challenges are less visible and require a trained eye to detect. Someone dealing with cash only is quite possibly economically fragile. For example, we had a teammate who moved her residence and was putting her children into a new school. During the move, the children's birth certificates were lost. Our teammate had to go to the state agency in person and pay cash to get the birth certificates.

Economically fragile people may have a history of repeated overdrafts, making it impossible to get a bank account. Or they may have poor credit that makes getting a credit card impossible.

Garnishment orders for low-wage earners can indicate economic fragility. The garnishment results in the employee not having as much money in their paycheck as they otherwise would, when every dollar is required to pay for basic living expenses.

Failure to enroll in company benefit programs is often another sign of economic fragility. Low-wage, economically fragile workers cannot afford to pay basic living expenses with more deductions from their paycheck. This, of course, leads to more risk in their lives, knowing that when something happens, they will not have the resources to manage it.

Enrollment in the Supplemental Nutritional Assistance Program (SNAP), formerly known as the food stamp program, indicates economic fragility. SNAP, funded by the federal government and administered by state government human services agencies, provides monthly subsidies via an Electronic Benefit Transfer card, which recipients use to purchase foods at local grocery stores and farmers markets. These benefits are not cash and can be used only on food purchases. SNAP benefits help supplement an individual's or a family's income to help buy nutritious food. Most households must spend some of their own cash along with their SNAP benefits to buy the food they need.

Another sign of economic fragility is enrollment in the Children's Health Insurance Program (CHIP). CHIP provides low-cost health coverage to children whose families earn too much money to qualify for Medicaid. CHIP benefits are different in each state. But all states provide comprehensive coverage, including routine check-ups, immunizations, doctor visits, prescriptions, dental and vision care, inpatient and outpatient hospital care, laboratory and X-ray services, and emergency services.

Employers often have to provide enrollment information for people to prove eligibility for SNAP and CHIP benefits. Company leadership may be unaware that their employees are utilizing these state and federal benefits that their human resources or accounting staff are helping to facilitate.

Another sign pointing to someone being economically fragile is their degree of access to high-speed internet and advanced telecommunications services, also known as broadband. While the 2013-2017 ACS estimates show overall widespread subscription to the internet throughout the country—78 percent of households nationally—the same statistics also show significantly lower subscription rates in rural and lower-income counties, at only 65 percent.[10]

While water and electricity reach almost all households, this is not the case for broadband internet. This "digital divide" is sizable and splits those who have and those who do not have access to high-speed internet. Workers without ready access to broadband at home may have to pay higher prices to use broadband sources available in stores. They may have children who are doing web-based homework at fast food restaurants where Wi-Fi is free.

The Flat Tire Catastrophe

Low-wage, economically fragile workers deal regularly with problems and issues that would immediately overwhelm many of us. As employers, most of us live a fairly routine and well-ordered life. It can come as quite a shock to us that some of our employees are serving our customers while they worry about where they are going to get affordable food, how they are going to get to work, and what to do with their children because the cash-only day care center just called and said that their children cannot come there anymore because they are not paying promptly. Imagine yourself in such a situation. What would you do? How would you manage?

The classic example of an economically fragile person is someone who has a flat tire. For many of us, a flat tire is merely an annoyance or an inconvenience. For someone who is economically fragile, a flat tire can be a genuine catastrophe, an unexpected expense setting off a chain reaction that can lead to food insecurity, housing insecurity, and transportation insecurity.

As they look at that flat tire, an economically fragile person knows they may end up missing work that day. If they can't get to work, they miss a day's wages. And they need every dollar from every work day. Losing even one day's pay—not to mention the expense of repairing or replacing the tire—may mean that they are not able to pay their utility bill, or make their rent payment, or even put food on the table until their next payday.

If they miss the entire day of work, they may find themselves forced to choose among their bills, because there is not enough money to pay for the tire repair along with the rent and their other basic expenses. So they decide to delay payment of the utility bill.

Going forward, the situation caused by the flat tire worsens. Catching up on utility bills just in time to avoid shut off makes it impossible to pay the rent on time. Catching up on that unpaid rent quickly will be required to stave off eviction. All the while, the small amount of money left for groceries leads low-wage economically fragile workers to experience food insecurity.

What is Food Insecurity?

We concur wholeheartedly with Teresa Miller, Secretary, Commonwealth of Pennsylvania Department of Human Services, who said, "In reality, so many Pennsylvanians go to work or school and live their lives on stomachs filled with empty calories, or stomachs that are just empty. The great thing is that, together, we have so many opportunities to change that."[11]

Food insecurity is common for low-wage economically fragile workers. It typically occurs near the end of a pay period or when the unavoidable payment of an unanticipated expense has left too little money for food.

People with food insecurity are uncertain about whether they will have enough food for themselves and their family. Food deprivation—or more clearly, hunger—happens when the cost of basic groceries exceeds available funds.

Experiencing food insecurity and food deprivation is frustrating and humiliating for low-wage economically fragile workers. Imagine working all day, going home, and opening a refrigerator that is mostly empty because you have no money left to put anything in it. There are full-time, dedicated workers who face this demoralizing experience repeatedly.

What is Housing Insecurity?

Experiencing housing insecurity is not knowing where you and your family are going to sleep. Housing insecurity can range from homelessness—the immediate fear of not knowing where you will sleep tonight—to a looming threat of losing whatever housing you have now.

Safe, affordable, high quality housing is as rare as a unicorn for low-wage, economically fragile workers. Where housing for low-wage earners is affordable, it is either not safe or it is a long commute, which can make it difficult for low-wage earners to hold a job.

Affordable housing is often the most challenging problem for low-wage, economically fragile workers. Easy math will show one reason for it.

Experts recommend spending no more than 30 percent of gross income on housing. For a full-time worker who is paid $10 per hour, this amounts to spending no more than $520 per month for rent. According to RentData.org, rent in Pennsylvania ranges from $697 for a two-bedroom apartment in rural Juniata County to $1,266 for a two-bedroom unit in Philadelphia.[12] That is 40 percent of gross income in Juniata County and 80 percent of gross income in Philadelphia.

Even when affordable housing can be found, there are slumlords who disappear until the rent payment is due or charge for repairs that should be included in the rent.

The lack of affordable housing has more than a financial impact on workers. According to the Build Healthy Places Network, "The nearly one-fifth of Americans who live in low-income communities have fewer opportunities to achieve healthy and rewarding lives. Many of the root causes of poverty and poor health are the same, and the community development and health sectors have worked for decades to address these challenges. However, these two sectors have often worked separately, even when serving the same places and people."[13]

For low-wage economically fragile workers, a lack of affordable housing, especially close to the workplace, can contribute to transportation insecurity.

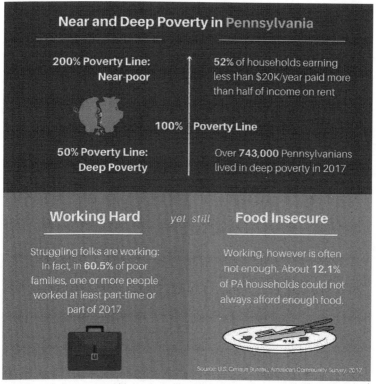

Near and Deep Poverty in Pennsylvania

200% Poverty Line: ↑ 52% of households earning
Near-poor less than $20K/year paid more
than half of income on rent

100% Poverty Line

50% Poverty Line: Over **743,000** Pennsylvanians
Deep Poverty lived in deep poverty in 2017

Working Hard *yet still* Food Insecure

Struggling folks are working: Working, however is often
In fact, in **60.5%** of poor not enough. About **12.1%**
families, one or more people of PA households could not
worked at least part-time or always afford enough food.
part of 2017

Source: U.S. Census Bureau, American Community Survey, 2017

Graphic courtesy of Community Action Association of Pennsylvania

What is Transportation Insecurity?

Experiencing transportation insecurity means not being sure—whatever your mode of transportation—that you will have a timely, reliable way to get to work and to the other places you and your family need to go.

Imagine not knowing when—or if—you can get to work or go food shopping or make a doctor's appointment. Having no control over your transportation makes scheduling impossible and day-to-day living chaotic.

Transportation insecurity can be the result of having no car, having an unreliable car, or sharing a car. It can also result from an inability to afford public transportation such as a bus or train, or lack of easy access to public transportation. Maybe the bus does not run consistently enough that you can count on it, or the schedule does not fit your work hours.

Managing the Insecurity

One of the common stereotypes about low-wage economically fragile workers is the belief that being economically fragile in the United States is optional. There is a frequent assumption that people who are economically fragile must be personally deficient somehow. They must be making bad choices or they must be irresponsible.

Economic fragility is by no means always the result of irresponsibility, and it is not necessarily a permanent condition. It may be a phase of life. There may be circumstances completely beyond the control of the individual that lead them to go from economic stability to economic fragility, or there may be circumstances that are part of a long traumatic personal history. The truth is that the economically fragile are a very diverse group of people with widely varying personal challenges.

"Why don't they just get a job?" is a question commonly asked about people on Medicaid. According to the most recent enrollment data, 60 percent of adults receiving Medicaid work full time (See "Understanding the Intersection of Medicaid and Work," Kaiser Family Foundation, 2018).[14]

We also heard many times over that the best social policy is a family-sustaining job. Leila Janah, author of *Give Work*, proved that dignified, family-sustaining work is indeed more effective in lifting people out of poverty than any aid program because it enables people to experience the kind of freedom, adventure, and independence that people with money take for granted. She demonstrated that work experience and training acquired in meaningful jobs provide the most effective avenue to prosperity.[15] However, families whose income is not yet sufficient for financial security must continually deal with the crises that result from inadequate resources. As we developed the *Team Member Prosperity and Success Model,* we came to the conclusion that it is narrow thinking to assume that the experience of employees when they are actually on the job is the only concern for a business.

Instead of pondering who was responsible to mitigate these risks for our employees, at Dasher we looked for explanations about why these risks existed for certain employees. One of those explanations, common in the health care industry, is the Social Determinants of Health (SDOH). According to the World Health Organization:

The SDOH are the conditions in which people are born, grow, live and work, and age. These circumstances are shaped by the distribution of money, power, and resources at global, national, and local levels. The SDOH are mostly responsible for health inequities—the unfair and avoidable difference in health status seen within and between countries.[16]

In other words, your zip code is more influential than your genetic code when it comes to overall health and life expectancy. People living in contiguous zip codes can have drastically different average health status. As we pondered how this slight difference in location could have been unnoticeable to us, we learned that this is apparent to people living in a zip code with lower life expectancy. Here is a telling statement that we heard: "We can see the other world even though the other world can't see us."

Our learning process also helped the Dasher leadership to take a new perspective on the work of community service organizations. For years, community service organizations have been attempting to mitigate the problems faced by low-wage, economically fragile workers.

For example, ALICE, an acronym created by the United Way in New Jersey, is just beginning to draw attention. It stands for Asset Limited Income Constrained Employed, and it refers to a demographic of workers.[17]

The definition of ALICE is men and women who have jobs and live above the federal poverty limit, but whose income is too low to create financial stability. They are workers who are dependent on hourly wages to pay for food and housing, those for whom a mechanical problem or a flat tire can be a genuine catastrophe.

In the next chapter, The Dasher Story, we explain our learning process as well as our motivation.

Chapter 2

The Dasher Story: A Brief History

IN 2008, DASHER WAS A SMALL, DIRECT MAIL COMPANY sailing headlong into a sea change that would decimate the mass mailing industry. For a group of social entrepreneurs, the ensuing market turbulence appeared to be filled with opportunity. It energized and inspired us to transform Dasher into an organization that provides interpersonal communication in any form to help people live happy, healthy lives. We wanted to create a peaceful, respectful existence at Dasher that could have a ripple effect on our world.

Transforming a small business firmly established in a rapidly declining industry is an adventure requiring a high tolerance for financial risk. Our business had debt, and our cash was limited. Despite our best efforts, not everything worked as planned.

The Great Recession took its toll on Dasher in 2009. We persevered, and in 2010, we began growing again. We had a much better understanding of how to manage our business financially and an even stronger desire to transform Dasher. And, as it turned out, we needed every ounce of that newly acquired knowledge and desire.

In August 2011, floodwaters from Hurricane Irene, a large and destructive storm on the East Coast of the United States, engulfed Dasher's building. Much of our equipment and office furniture was destroyed. Our losses were in the hundreds of thousands of dollars.

The power of Mother Nature is something we will never forget. Electrical service was cut off to prevent fire. In the darkness, our team waded in river water mixed with sewage trying to salvage what we could. This included supplies, files, and pictures of children from our teammates' desks.

First and foremost, we still give thanks that no one on our team was injured. We retrieved the computer server just before it was submerged. That server kept Dasher's heart beating while our clients and our central Pennsylvania community made it possible for us to recover.

We faced many other business storms that all seemed like death blows at first but turned out to be valuable lessons. Despite serious financial pressures and continuous shifts in the markets Dasher serves, we remained committed social entrepreneurs. We learned that being a values-driven business is what enables us to be a profitable business. From the beginning and to this day, we continuously ask ourselves what kind of positive social impact we can have that will support our core business.

As we were changing our service delivery model, we tied everything we did to helping people live happy, healthy lives.

This is our mission: to help people live happy, healthy lives. What do we mean by that? Others will have their own definitions; we've given a lot of thought to ours. We believe that "healthy" means a person is in balance. It means that mind, body, and spirit all receive nourishment and focus.

"Happy," of course, can and will differ from person to person. We consider it to be the ability and the freedom to follow your dream—whatever that dream may be—and also the ability to be who you are. We understand that there are many, many ways to define "happy, healthy life." But when we say that we want to help people live happy, healthy lives, this is what we mean.

As we looked internally at Dasher, we gradually realized that many of our cherished teammates who were in low-wage jobs had serious life challenges rooted in economic fragility. We became passionate—and we are still passionate—about working with economically fragile people and creating access to prosperity for them.

Our passion for working with low-wage, economically fragile people ended up driving the transformation we envisioned in 2008. We worked systematically to be a successful, for-profit business that invests the time and money to attract, engage, retain, and create opportunities to thrive for low-wage, economically fragile workers. People familiar with the Dasher business model 10 years ago are astounded and often comment that we are a totally different company. Eureka!

Today, Dasher is a small business that is fiscally disciplined, financially strong, and exists to help people live happy, healthy lives. This applies to both our clients and our employees. Our number one priority is to deliver a customer experience that makes working with us attractive and productive. There is not one minute of one day when we forget that Dasher is a business providing client service.

With our *Team Member Prosperity and Success Model* in operation and getting measurable results, the optimal business opportunities for Dasher are those which create jobs for low-wage, economically fragile people and require precise execution with measurable results.

With a specialized knowledge of healthcare, Dasher communicates complex information via mail, text, email, telephone, and face-to-face communication. Dasher also has considerable experience with data management, data security, auto emissions, and professional licensure. These are complex subjects.

This is where the *Team Prosperity and Success Model* overlaps with our service delivery models. We are helping Dasher employees to change behaviors that are not helping them and to acquire other behaviors that will benefit them at Dasher and in their lives in general. We convey the desired behavior, why it is beneficial, and how to demonstrate that behavior.

In turn, our Dasher employees know very well how to communicate on behalf of our clients with the intent to change the behavior of people by conveying the desired behavior, why it is beneficial, and how to demonstrate that behavior. To produce positive results for clients, our team uses some of the same approaches that we use internally for communicating with the Dasher team.

Our clients range from global companies to small businesses and nonprofits. Anyone who wants to send a message reliably and effectively is a potential client for Dasher. We have many long-standing clients and they want to support Dasher because we get results and they can see for themselves firsthand, up close, that what we are doing is changing lives and helping people.

What we have sought to do with this book is describe our own journey and advocate for engaging with economically fragile workers. We view this as simply one path. We hope that many other successful approaches will emerge and that other models will be developed that create access to economic stability for our entire workforce.

When we started down this path, we had what now turns out to have been a simplistic view. Our learning came in seeing what it is to live with the stress, the lack of a safety net, and the day-to-day crises that are part of the reality of economically fragile people.

Over time, we realized that we had to go slowly, tread lightly, and go much broader and deeper in providing support for this talented group of people if we were going to help them actually achieve their goals and be successful.

There was no precedent or text book case study to follow, and in business, especially small business, it is risky to take a path that is not well traveled. At the time we embarked on this journey, the term "social entrepreneur" was not in common use in Harrisburg, Pennsylvania. We understood that we were not following what were commonly held to be "business rules," and we were putting Dasher's success in question.

To reach our objectives, we had to change our entire thought process and revamp our approach to doing business. We had to stop thinking Dasher was a direct mail company. We had to start learning how to make Dasher transform lives.

None of this is simple. But it is doable. The fact that Dasher is thriving today illustrates how a business can survive with committed leadership, imagination, and perseverance. We had a lot riding on this. We put the business at financial risk to test this model. It was never just some minor project that we tried. We staked our future on it.

Now here we are, 10 years later, going strong, and we are sharing a proven, financially successful process in a book that shows how employers can help low-wage, economically fragile workers become prosperous and economically stable, and lead happy, healthy lives. Life is so interesting!

As you read about the *Team Member Prosperity and Success Model*, you'll be meeting some of our team members and hearing in their own words about the very personal impact this model has had on them at work and in life.

Chapter 3

The Team Member
Prosperity and Success Model

TRUST.

None of what Dasher does is possible without trust, and that takes time to build. Working with low-wage economically fragile people starts with building trust. If we translated this into a math equation, it would be this:

Trust = Culture + Predictability

Culture is so important to us that we gave ours a name: The Dasher Way.

Dasher's predictability, clarity, and consistency come directly from implementation of our Dasher *Team Member Prosperity and Success Model*.

At Dasher, then, the equation becomes:

Trust = The Dasher Way + The Dasher Team Prosperity and Success Model

We will describe each of these components in detail

Developing Our Culture: The Dasher Way

In 2008, Dasher had a set of typically worded core values and a culture set by default. As part of our company transformation, we decided to change this. Today, our constant number one priority is delivering a customer experience that makes working with Dasher attractive and productive for clients.

Our culture, the Dasher Way, influences how we operate every facet of our business. It is all about getting to that end result. An essential ingredient for our culture is strong core values that are behaviorally defined and deeply embedded in all that we do. They are real, not aspirational.

The following is our process for making and sustaining this important culture change at Dasher. We aspired to be a tribe, as defined in Seth Godin's book, *Tribes*. As outlined in this very influential book, "a tribe is a group of people connected to one another, connected to a leader, and connected to an idea."[18]

In *Tribes*, Mr. Godin also points out that to be a tribe, it is necessary to have "a shared interest and a way to communicate."

As a first step, we thought about employees at Dasher who personified our commitment to deliver a customer experience that makes working with Dasher attractive and productive for our clients. If we could identify an ideal employee or a group of ideal employees, who would they be? We thought of those people and we asked, "What is it about these people that makes them so great for Dasher? Maybe they would not be so great for someone else's company, but why are they are great for us?"

By going through that process of thinking about those wonderful employees and what it was that made them so special to us, we came up with these values:

- Positivity
- Customer focus
- Caring and respect
- Accountability
- Able to learn
- Teamwork

Because we had teammates who already possessed these core values as evidenced by their work, we did not have to embark on an extensive campaign to change the behavior of our entire team to fit with aspirational (and possibly unrelatable) core values.

No matter how clear we considered our core values to be, we suspected that ambiguities would most likely erode attempts at living our core values. Exactly what is teamwork? What does it mean to be positive? We had to make it easy.

Our next step was to identify the specific behaviors we thought defined these core values. If someone on the Dasher team exhibited one or more of these behaviors, then that person would be demonstrating their adherence to that core value.

To identify those specific behaviors, we looked at a variety of sources, including lists of behaviors from many different companies. We looked for behaviors that other companies have identified as important for their employees, and from that list we culled the behaviors that we wanted to assign to each of our core values.

The sources of inspiration for Dasher's behaviors include the Ritz Carlton[19], the Dave Ramsey Organization[20], a wide variety of business websites, and the book *Fundamentally Different* by David Friedman, principal in High Performing Culture, LLC.[21]

Once we identified the values by thinking about our best people and identified the behaviors by going through this process of looking at all the many possibilities, we had the Dasher Way.

We created a visual representation of the Dasher Way, put it into a brochure, and shared it with our team after several weeks of lead-up discussions that prepared them for the introduction. We had a very intentional and important introduction to our employees about the Dasher Way and what it meant, with examples.

The Dasher Way is our shared set of norms, where everyone understands the rules the same way. This is the way we behave. It gives us a common language and a common way of being that is shared by every individual.

We don't lose sight of the fact that everybody is an individual. The Dasher Way (our culture) gives us a baseline that allows each person to be treated differently, as an individual, in accordance with their needs. We take this a step further, believing that long-term success depends on the celebration, validation, and respect of each individual, as an individual. For example, Dasher teammates living in accordance with our behaviors and core values can be emotional, colorful, outgoing, introverted, a fashionista, Goth, perpetually casual, reserved, laid back, all business, a dreamer, a thinker, a jokester, a hugger, a seeker, and any personality type.

To make sure that everyone continues to focus on the Dasher Way, we have produced in-house every single week since the introduction, an email and an entertaining, 90-second video that addresses one of the behaviors. It started with our senior team, and now our teammates are jumping in front of the camera as well as directing the videos.

Each video is about four questions:

1. What is the value/behavior?
2. What is one way to show a commitment to that value/behavior?
3. Why is it good to behave this way?
4. How does living the value/behavior help the employee, our customers, and Dasher?

The weekly video is shown again at our weekly staff meetings, and we have people talking about examples of that behavior that they have seen in our workplace. The examples are often numerous and inspiring.

The weekly video is part of our continual dripping—repeating positive behaviors and messages over and over so they become second nature to everyone on the team. We are constantly dripping on people relative to Dasher's culture.

For example, one of the behaviors in the Dasher Way is "Never Gossip." Gossip is absolutely not permitted at Dasher. This zero tolerance promotes trust that is essential for the implementation of the *Team Member Prosperity and Success Model*. Prohibiting gossip helps to create a nurturing environment for people because they can share open and honest dialogue that is helpful to everybody. They know they are not going to get stabbed in the back. They know that people are not going to be talking about them or taking pleasure from their challenges.

We reap the benefits of the never gossip policy. People feel safe. It increases the level of trust. There are fewer secrets. People help each other with the challenges that they face. They can trust each other to say, "Hey, I have this problem," and know somebody will respond with, "Oh, yeah. I did too. Here is how you fix that."

We go beyond talking about our culture by rewarding employees for demonstrating the behaviors identified in the Dasher Way. In essence, we try very hard to catch people doing things right. This creates a nurturing culture that promotes team health. We explain more about our internally-developed "Gotcha" reward program in Chapter 10 on Leadership.

Developing Our Model: Team Member Prosperity and Success

Dasher has many proven processes, some for very complex services, each illustrated as a single-page flowchart. As we have started to talk to clients about what Dasher is doing, we saw value in illustrating what we do to enable our Dasher team members to be successful in the same kind of process picture that Dasher has for all the other services that we offer.

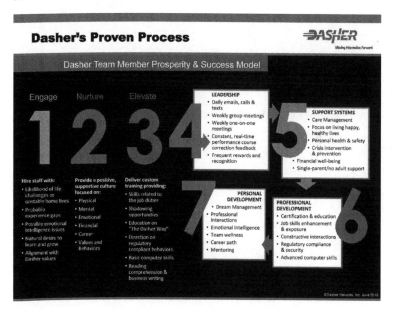

Dasher's *Team Member Prosperity and Success Model* depicts a seven-step process that guides how Dasher recruits, hires, supports, and interacts with employees to provide them with the opportunity to be prosperous and successful on their own terms as well as ours. This and subsequent chapters will look in detail at the steps of this process.

We often are asked about the return on investment of the *Team Member Prosperity and Success Model*. At Dasher, we measure several key performance indicators on a quarterly basis, including revenue, net income from operations, revenue per FTE, and the ratio of benefit costs to salaries.

These quantitative measures of Dasher's financial performance serve as one part of our ongoing evaluation of the *Team Member Prosperity and Success Model*. We also consider direct costs for implementation of the model, some of which are nonrecurring (such as labor required to develop Lunch 'N Learns, and the costs for non-traditional benefits, such as our Gotcha program, our Employee Fund, and our Starter Emergency Funds) or recurring expenses (such as changes in personnel, supplies, and materials or maintenance and repair). Whenever possible, we view our efforts in monetary terms to facilitate the assessment of a project's net value.

In addition to numerical measurement, we also consider the potential impact of not implementing the model and while this is subjective, we have concluded to date that the model offers value to our entire enterprise in the form of higher morale, employee retention, and dedication to our clients.

Measuring Outcomes

For each business function occurring at Dasher, we have separate scorecards to track weekly performance of our processes, including finance, marketing, production, and contact center operations. Likewise, we also have a scorecard for the *Team Member Prosperity and Success Model*. What our management team deems to be key performance indicators on each scorecard are recorded on a company scorecard and reviewed and discussed weekly in Dasher's senior management team meeting.

The scorecard for the *Team Member Prosperity and Success Model* is shown here.

2019 - Dasher Team Member Prosperity & Success Model Metrics

	Goal
ENGAGE	
Unplanned Turnover	0/month
Number of Open Positions	<=1
NURTURE	
Participation in Wellness Practices	50% of staff
ELEVATE	
Attendance at Lunch & Learns	75% of staff
Timesheet Errors	<=2/month
LEADERSHIP	
Gotcha Nominations	4/month
SUPPORT SYSTEMS	
Lost Days Due to Unplanned Absences	3/month
PROFESSIONAL DEVELOPMENT	
Human Caused Quality Events	0/month
Production Projects Overdue	0/month
Calls Answered Within 90 Seconds	80%
PERSONAL DEVELOPMENT	
Smart Dollar Points Earned	5,000/month
Active Starter Emergency Fund Participation	75%

To measure the success of each step of the model, Dasher tracks specific outcomes from each step of the *Team Member Prosperity and Success Model.* By continually monitoring and analyzing the results, the executive leadership team knows where to dedicate time and effort in developing new strategies and otherwise taking steps to improve the outcome.

On the next page is our data dictionary for these measures. In succeeding chapters, we explain programs in more detail as noted in the description of the measure.

Data Dictionary

Unplanned Turnover: A monthly count of employees who have resigned.

Number of Open Positions: A monthly count of the open positions that are actively being filled.

Participation in Wellness Practices: (Chapter 5) A monthly calculation of the number of people attending each session divided by the possible/available employees in the office who could attend.

Attendance at Lunch 'N Learn Sessions: (Chapter 5) A monthly calculation of the number of employees that attend a paid opportunity for lunch and learn divided by the possible/available employees who could attend. (Also calculated by session to measure topical appeal.)

Timesheet Errors: A monthly calculation of the number of timesheet errors submitted after review by all supervisors.

Gotcha Nominations: (Chapter 7) The total number of Gotcha nominations made each month.

Lost Days Due to Unplanned Absences: Total number of days lost due to employee call-offs no matter what the reason. Scheduled Personal Time Off (PTO) is not included in this calculation. (Also calculated weekly for real time management of issues that arise.)

Human Caused Quality Events: A monthly count of errors that occur in the production area that are triggered by a human touch, not solely machine triggered. (Also calculated weekly to facilitate debrief and procedure correction as needed.)

Production Projects Overdue: A count of production projects that exceed the contract defined service level agreements for each client. (Also calculated weekly to facilitate debrief and procedure correction as needed.)

Calls Answered Within 90 Seconds: A review of call center activity where the goal is to answer 80 percent of all calls within 90 seconds. (This metric is calculated continuously by our phone system and also reviewed daily and weekly to facilitate debrief and procedure correction as needed.)

SmartDollar™ Points Earned: (Chapter 5) The points earned by the enrolled staff per month.

Active Starter Emergency Fund Participation: (Chapter 5) The total number of individual employee-owned starter emergency fund bank accounts divided by the total number of eligible employees.

For each measure, we set a goal and track results monthly or more frequently as needed. With more than 50 employees as of this writing, it is easy to see that some of our goals may not be applicable to larger businesses. Dasher's goal for unplanned turnover is zero! Our goal for participation in Dasher's Starter Emergency Fund is 75 percent and actual participation is currently even higher. For an employer 100 times our size, initial goals are likely to be much different.

Of great importance to us are the measured results we seek from the *Team Member Prosperity and Success Model* that impact clients. Timesheet errors threaten the accuracy of client billing and cost center financial analysis, and we teach extensively about the importance of tracking time accurately. Human-caused quality events, lost work days, and call center performance impact Dasher's ability to complete projects on time and correctly. We utilize the scorecard constantly to determine areas for improvement in the *Team Member Prosperity and Success Model.*

Dasher's *Team Member Prosperity and Success Model* could not function effectively without the Dasher Way, our culture, being thoroughly ingrained. It is integrated throughout the process, including hiring, training, evaluating, coaching, and rewarding as we will examine step-by-step in the chapters ahead.

As we review the *Team Member Prosperity and Success Model* in detail, it will become clear that preserving dignity and establishing deep relationships with each individual start even before someone is hired. It will also be apparent that the model requires intentional effort and dedication of resources over time.

For example, a Dasher client observed, "We love the results you are getting for us and the services you are providing for us. Could we engage Dasher to train our employees to perform as well as your employees?"

Our client was not trying to replace Dasher with their own team. Understandably, they just wanted to get the same excellent results from their low-wage workers. After reviewing the *Team Member*

Prosperity and Success Model, our client agreed with our conclusion that it was not training, it was the entire system.

Putting the model on paper has also been a tool to gain the commitment of the entire executive leadership team, which is important because the most effective change comes from the top down. It requires a persistent, consistent, sustained effort on the part of the CEO and the senior leadership team.

Voices of Dasher

Melissa is a community healthcare supervisor at Dasher, a single mom of a young son, and an active volunteer with several nonprofit organizations.

Her many volunteer activities include an annual mission trip to Haiti. The annual trip was supposed to take place shortly after she joined Dasher almost two years ago, but as a new employee she hadn't yet accumulated vacation time to take the trip. Melissa was astonished when her brand-new employer donated the week so that she could still make the trip, supporting her passion for making the world a better place.

Melissa says:

Dasher donated that week to me so that I could still do something that was really important to me. . . .

The core values that we have here at Dasher are really important because those are the same core values that I have in my personal life. It's nice to be able to not have to switch my focus when I'm at work. I can still focus on helping people and being passionate and learning and continuing to do the things I love—and getting paid to do them. It's not just our clients that get empowered and have better lives. We get to have better lives as well. . . .

I just really appreciate being able to come to work every day. . . . I feel like I am valued as a person and not just for what I can do while I'm here. Of course it's important that I do my job, but I am truly valued as an entire human being and for the things I do both inside and outside of work.

Chapter 4

The Dasher Model: Engage

THE FIRST STEP in the Dasher *Team Member Prosperity and Success Model* is Engage. We define engagement as identifying and hiring talent who can succeed in the organization while contributing to Dasher's ongoing success.

Hiring at Dasher

Dasher's hiring process consists of identifying candidates, interviewing, testing, and selection. The steps in our process are common. How we implement the steps to identify and hire talented economically fragile teammates is regulatory-compliant and may differ from generally-accepted practice.

You may ask why Dasher spends this much time and effort hiring low-wage, economically fragile workers. We do it to protect our culture and to maximize employee retention. Using the hiring process we describe, Dasher's employee turnover last year was just 10 percent, well below industry averages for our sector of 30 to 40 percent.

Identifying Candidates

What makes a qualified candidate? First and foremost, Dasher looks for people whose personal values align with the Dasher Way. If they do not, it is a non-starter. If somebody seems perfect in every other way and there is a values issue, the discussion ends right there. We always acknowledge people and thank them for their time and interest. It is good karma.

Along with values alignment, our candidates must have a passion to learn and grow. We take a calculated risk, knowing that their alignment with the Dasher Way and their natural desire to learn predict they will thrive within Dasher's *Team Member Prosperity and Success Model*. For example, Dasher is open to taking a chance on a candidate who may lack a high school diploma, when we can see from their track record that with support, they are likely to finish a GED.

With our focus on low-income, economically fragile workers, we expect to find people who have life challenges, trauma, past or present instability in their home lives, experience gaps, educational gaps, and possibly emotional intelligence issues. We are not deterred by such things because we are prepared to help our people find their own resilience and strengths.

We focus on the person and not the superficial package. Dasher welcomes candidates who may be covered in tattoos, sport multiple piercings, or have fanciful hairstyles that do not fit a corporate look, focusing our attention strictly on their capabilities. One of our clients had to make an exception to a tattoo policy in their workplace when we delivered highly capable employees to work onsite; they now greatly respect and appreciate the quality of their work.

When we are recruiting, our Dasher job postings include less information about our wants and needs and more about the benefits to candidates from working for Dasher. We communicate how it feels to be a member of our team and explain how Dasher supports the achievement of personal goals and dreams.

We point potential candidates to our Facebook page, our LinkedIn company page, and our website because each of those, particularly our Facebook page, illustrates from a different perspective what it is like to be at Dasher and what makes us different, starting with the Dasher Way.

Dasher's website includes videos and discussions about our values. Our online image shows potential candidates our employee-centric workplace and how being part of our company means taking part in our mission of helping people lead happy, healthy lives. The mission focus of the organization appeals strongly to the types of candidates that Dasher wants to attract.

To find candidates, Dasher partners with the county workforce development office, as well as workforce training organizations. Our referral sources send top candidates to us because they know we move quickly in the hiring process, communicate extensively throughout to aid in finding the right person, and treat the people we hire in a way that will enable their success.

We also use non-relationship-based candidate sources such Craigslist and social media. There are many candidates on Craigslist who are diverse in every way.

We actively seek personal referrals. People who know Dasher know how great it is to work here, so they refer their friends, neighbors, colleagues from previous jobs, kids, even their parents. Convinced that good people herd together, the leadership team relishes the opportunity to consider candidates sent our way by people we know.

The hiring team starts talking to potential candidates without formalities or paperwork. At an appropriate point, every candidate completes a straight-forward application.

One of our mottoes is: Always be recruiting! Our team is constantly looking for and thinking about talent. If a good candidate comes along, we engage them and talk about current opportunities and future opportunities. They can even work for us on a temporary project—even if we have to create one—so that we can get to know a promising person.

The Interview Process

Once we have identified a potential candidate, then the direct supervisor for the available position reviews all available information—including the potential candidate's social media posts—to decide if this is someone we want to get to know and if they qualify for an interview by telephone.

Lasting 30-45 minutes, the telephone interview usually involves two people asking a very specific set of questions. These questions are tightly focused to look for alignment with our values and a natural desire to learn and grow.

Here are some of Dasher's telephone screening questions:

- Tell me about a time when you had an assignment and were stumped. What did you do?
- Tell me about a time when you experienced conflict with a fellow employee. What did you do?
- Tell me about a time when you had too much to do.
- Tell me about a time when you had not enough to do.
- Tell me about a time when you made a mistake.

At Dasher, our philosophy is that qualified candidates who are aligned with the Dasher Way are precious. We do not wait to find two or three other candidates to move to the next step, which is an in-depth, in-person interview.

Dasher's interview process was inspired by the book *Hiring Talent: Decoding Levels of Work in the Behavioral Interview* by Tom Foster.[22] Using this game-changing book, we developed a substantial bank of questions—they address all the values, the passion for learning and growing, and specific job requirements. There are no hypothetical questions in the list. Hypothetical responses are not reliable, they do not generate useful information, and we do not allow them.

Each promising candidate is invited to spend about 90 minutes with us. Two Dasher leaders will probe more deeply using a prescribed set of questions that delve into specific things for which the candidate has been accountable, real experiences the candidate has had, and actual results the candidate has delivered.

Here are some of our interview questions:

Describe a decision you have made recently that had an important effect on you.

How did you go about it?

How has it turned out?

How did you involve others?

Tell us about a recent change you experienced at work. Was it a good idea or bad idea and why?

Talk about something you had to get done, and you didn't know how to do it.

How have you helped someone recently?

Tell me about a time when things didn't go the way you wanted.

Tell me about a time when you needed to lead others to get something done.

Tell me about a time when you missed an important goal.

When we say, "Tell us about a time when you missed an important goal," we do not want to hear, "Well, if I were to miss a goal, I would do this." We repeat, "Tell us about a time when you actually did miss an important goal. Why was it important? What exactly was the situation? How did it happen? What was your particular role in that situation? What did you do? What actions did you take? What was the result? What specifically did you learn?"

If a candidate responds, "I never missed a goal," that is useful information. It may signal the inability to embrace accountability—a red flag that there is likely to be a values mismatch. Everybody misses goals! And when they do, we expect our team to own it.

Recently we were hiring for a position in which writing skills are important, along with seeking and incorporating feedback about the work, and meeting tight deadlines. After sharing details about the job opportunity, we asked the interviewees to rewrite their resumes to present a more compelling picture of why Dasher should hire them. We asked for delivery to us the next day.

It was a very effective way of distinguishing candidates: one candidate came through with flying colors, and another could not figure out why we asked them to do it. That was all we needed to discern that one person was a fit for us and that the other was not aligned with the Dasher Way.

Final Steps in Hiring

If the interview goes well, we check references immediately. For most hires, Dasher also has a testing process to understand personality traits directly related to the Dasher Way, such as positivity and accountability. While we glean a great deal out of the interview, we want to get to the next layer below by using a consistent testing process. For some jobs, such as those requiring a relatively higher level of cognitive skill, we will administer a cognitive test as well.

While there are several testing approaches used in hiring, Dasher utilizes the Assess Personality Survey to learn about a candidate's core competencies and Prevue Learning & Reasoning to better understand our candidates' pace for processing information and capacity for handling complexity and ambiguity.

On the combined basis of the first two interviews and the test results, we determine which candidates will meet with someone on the executive leadership team along with the hiring manager. There are two people in the meeting, sometimes more, for a variety of points of view. We have additional prescribed questions designed to bring out more experiences and behavioral examples in areas that the preceding steps have highlighted for further exploration.

Following that meeting, the group together decides whether the candidate is qualified on all counts. If they are the right person for Dasher, we get an offer out to them within a day.

From the time a promising resume comes in until we make an offer can be as little as seven days. We move at lightning speed to evaluate and hire candidates who are a fit for Dasher before they have a chance to think about working anywhere else.

We always acknowledge people and thank them, whether or not we choose to pursue them as a candidate. While they may not be a fit for us and our culture, they may well be perfect for another organization. We believe that everybody has a place.

Chapter 5

The Dasher Model: Nurture

DASHER'S NURTURING ENVIRONMENT helps our team members create a life outside of work that enables them to come to work and thrive. They can be productive and successful in an atmosphere where they can do their best and achieve what matters most to them. It is like providing fertile soil for seeds to grow.

Our nurturing environment is comprised of compensation and traditional benefits along with an ever-growing variety of non-traditional benefits that help our team to live healthy lives and support their families.

Supportive, Safe, Respectful

Dasher's safe environment encourages people to seek help themselves and to help one another without fear of experiencing shame or diminishment. Our team can trust that Dasher will not put them in a situation where they are not being treated with the same caring and respect that we expect them to demonstrate to others. We never expect Dasher teammates to stay in situations where they are not treated respectfully in any of the many ways we interact with people. To do so would destroy our nurturing environment.

For example, inbound callers to Dasher's contact center are seeking assistance in dealing with a variety of stressful situations. The callers may be upset and angry. We train our contact center teammates how to show respect for the callers' state of mind and how to gain respect from callers who are initially disrespectful.

Following is the text of an email that illustrates this point about creating mutual respect. It was sent to one of Dasher's contact center representatives, who was assisting a caller with a complex process of getting a temporary professional cosmetology license:

From: **********@aol.com
Sent: Thursday, January 17, 2019 1:18 PM
To: *********@dasherinc.com
Subject: RE: Temp
Hello _____! I just wanted to reach out and thank you again for going the extra mile to help me resolve my situation and finally get my temp license. I wish there were more people like yourself. My family and I Thank you so very much. When I got the email I printed it out drove to my wifes salon handed it to her with tears of joy running down my face. I can seriously say had it not been for you dealing with me being a pain in the ass I would still be lost wandering what's next. God Bless you and your family, _____ , and thank you forever.

Compensation and Traditional Benefits

Dasher offers competitive wages that are generally above the market, expecting to reap a return from reduced turnover. We teach employees how to understand their pay information, working with them to evaluate all deductions so they are able to confirm that correct amounts are being withheld.

Traditional benefits include health, disability, vision, and dental insurance; 401K with a generous match; and paid time off. Dasher pays a substantial portion of the cost of traditional benefits so that our employees can afford to opt for insurance coverage. We take exceptional care to make sure that the insurance coverage requires modest out-of-pocket participation so that employees can use their benefits to be as healthy as possible.

Senior leaders at Dasher invest time in educating the team about health insurance—teaching how to access all of the benefits the insurers offer; how to shop for healthcare; and how to maximize insurer reimbursements and minimize their cost by using networks, approved labs, generic options, telemedicine, and urgent care rather than the emergency department.

Dasher provides the full benefits package to full-time employees and part-time employees who work at least 24 hours a week, guaranteeing Dasher an advantage in attracting and retaining part-time workers.

Non-Traditional Benefits

Dasher's non-traditional benefits address financial wellness along with the wellbeing of the whole person. It is one thing to offer these non-traditional benefits; it is another thing entirely to persuade our team to accept and embrace them. The non-traditional benefits, seemingly generous, facilitate their personal growth. But in essence, these benefits are asking people to change behavior.

Changing behavior is uncomfortable for everyone, especially for people who have had negative life experiences that naturally lead them to be suspicious of change. To overcome the inertia that comes from negative past experiences, we seek ways to make behavior change less intimidating.

We make a compelling offer based on how the benefit helps our team, and we repeat it frequently. We offer tangible incentives for trying the healthy behavior. We demonstrate what we mean by modeling the behavior over and over.

Knowing that many of our team are skeptical, we expect to see success a bit at a time. We embrace the challenge of finding what else we can do that will promote health and wellness for the whole person. Persistence, patience, respect, and curiosity on our part are all essential parts of the equation.

A key financial wellness tool that we provide at no cost to employees is SmartDollar™, an online financial wellness program[23] providing video lessons, real-world content applications, and a team of experts, including Dave Ramsey, who teach how to manage money. With SmartDollar™, our teammates get free access to a step-by-step plan that has worked for millions of people. Our team is learning how to budget, save, pay off debt, and invest.

The first of seven baby steps in SmartDollar™ is saving $1,000 for a Starter Emergency Fund, which is money that a person saves for those unexpected events that occur in everyone's lives. These dollars can be generated by having a budget that includes dollars for savings and creating additional household income through yard sales and such.

We learned from talking to our team that many did not embrace budgeting. They said budgeting is for people who have money, not for them. Many also saw it as out of reach because it is too complicated.

Dasher leadership took this feedback seriously and did some research. According to one source, 65 percent of Americans cannot cover a $1,000 emergency—that is two-thirds of all people.[24] And nearly half of all Americans—46 percent—cannot cover a $400 emergency, according to a Federal Reserve study.[25]

Understanding the resistance to budgeting and critical need for having a Starter Emergency Fund led us to take three steps.

First, we provided cash rewards to anybody who was willing to track their monthly expenses, use this information to put together a budget, and then implement their budget using an envelope system, a top way for people with limited cash to get spending under control.

Second, Dasher helped each employee to open a Starter Emergency Fund bank account. We make the first deposit into their account, and add more after-tax dollars periodically as they reach interim savings goals. In one year, an employee can have a $1,000 Starter Emergency Fund.

Third, we developed a practical (and fun) how-to-budget seminar geared to low-income people and had almost 100 percent attendance.

We continue to promote SmartDollar™ to our team on a weekly basis and watch online videos in groups. As of today, 80 percent of Dasher employees are enrolled.

Dasher Wellness Practice

Another non-traditional benefit that Dasher offers is a daily routine—tailored to an uninitiated, skeptical audience—for helping to inspire happiness and reduce stress. We refer to it as the Dasher Wellness Practice. Twice each day, all Dasher employees can stop working and join together as a group for Wellness Practice. The Dasher Wellness Practice is structured and predictable. It has four components done in the same order every time: meditation, thinking of others, writing in a gratitude journal, and movement. No component lasts more than two minutes.

In line with Dasher's belief in repeatedly modeling healthy behavior, we started with our leaders, doing these practices daily in a conference room with windows so that anyone walking by could see us meditating, jumping up and down, and writing together in a book. After a few weeks of consistent practice, we asked the team if they would like to know what we were doing. People were curious.

Over time, as we developed this practice, we have taught people the how as well as the why, explaining the benefits behind each of these components. Each teammate now has their own gratitude journal, a gift from Dasher. While we model, teach, and repeat, no one is forced to participate.

Now our Wellness Practice is ingrained, occurring twice a day. We start by ringing a bell; it resonates around the office and almost makes you relax as soon as you hear it. That sound reminds everyone to meditate, think good thoughts, express gratitude, and move. We have invited others to lead the Wellness Practice, creating leadership opportunities for people at a low threshold, where they can practice leading a group in the least intimidating way. It is an easily accessible chance to lead something that they know Dasher leaders have said is very important.

To illustrate the skepticism which any new ideas must overcome in order to be adopted in a group of economically fragile (and risk-averse) people, consider what prevented one of our team from embracing Dasher Wellness Practice. We initially introduced this brief group time together with the name Dasher Wellness Rituals. A member of our team associates rituals with evil anti-religious practices bringing harm to innocent people, and so she understandably refused to participate. Reminded once again of how different our perceptions are, based on our diversity of past experiences, we changed the name, and she was able to embrace Wellness Practice.

We believe these group activities help us to share a common language and a way of being together. It's not somebody saying, "You should do this and you should do that." It is a shared experience that generates connection and also a shared understanding of a good way to live.

Sustaining a Nurturing Environment

Nurturing our employees through a keen emphasis on wellness of the whole person is important to our overall focus on helping economically fragile employees to thrive. And that leads us to Step Three in our *Team Member Prosperity and Success Model*, which is Elevate.

Voices of Dasher

Gabrielle, an outbound call center team leader, has been with Dasher for eight years. She has faced many obstacles in her quest to provide her children with safe, stable housing, a caring environment, decent food, and quality education. Managing finances has been especially difficult for Gabrielle, given her lack of an emergency fund, chronic health issues, and high housing costs that eat up a precariously large portion of her income. Little, if any, training about how to handle money and a lack of support from her family have only contributed to her challenges.

Offered the chance to make a 90-second video about some aspect of the Dasher Way to share with the whole team, Gabrielle agreed to do so. Unprompted, Gabrielle opted to talk about SmartDollar™ and Dasher's Starter Emergency Fund.

Gabrielle says:

Dasher has already helped us jumpstart our emergency fund. How about if we share some information with you on budgeting which may help you grow your emergency fund even more? Every dollar should have a place and we will show you how.

I actually started using the envelope system with the help of Mrs. Cyndi. To my surprise, it actually worked and will for you too if you are dedicated to what you are doing.

To begin, you must write out your budget. Then you'll need to label each envelope with your expenses.

Let's just say our budget each month is $1400.

This is the money I have to use to cover my expenses:

Rent which is $500

Food for the month at $300

Utilities should be about $200

Children expenses $200

Car items at $100

Home supplies, which could be miscellaneous items for about $100.

Sometimes, to feel more confident, you just need to hear real life experiences. Sharing information is a great way to let someone know that they are not alone!

Chapter 6

The Dasher Model: Elevate

STEP THREE OF Dasher's *Team Member Prosperity and Success Model*, Elevate, goes hand in hand with the nurturing environment described in the previous chapter. This chapter reviews the education and training Dasher provides to team members to prepare them for their roles.

Dasher equips our low-wage, economically fragile workers with the skills they will need to become economically stable by structuring its learning experience carefully and delivering the training in a way our employees are likely to absorb to maximize success.

While the acquisition of general and job-specific skills makes our teammates good employees for anyone, not just Dasher, it also makes them less likely to decide to leave. Sometimes people will move on to better opportunities based on their personal dreams and goals, and we wish them well. Most people, however, want to stay.

Dasher makes them feel valued through the investments we make in them and the environment of dignity and respect that we create. When employees feel valued and part of an environment that promotes their wellbeing and success, chances are that they will make the choice to stay.

We have come to understand that economically fragile people do not necessarily come to the workplace looking for training. They may not have had good learning experiences in school or in past training situations, so we cannot just expect them to immediately embrace each and every training opportunity. That is why we go beyond delivering training that meets the company's needs to focusing on the needs of the whole person—what is important to our teammates and what their goals are. Of course we care that they have general professional skills and job-related skills, but we also care about their health, their wellbeing, their financial security, and their happiness. We offer learning opportunities in every one of these categories, often through what we call Lunch 'N Learn sessions.

For example, we brought in a personal trainer to talk about exercise and nutrition. Once a week we have a brief fitness class taught by one of our teammates who is a certified Refit instructor. On another occasion we brought in a police officer to talk about personal safety—how to keep yourself safe in various situations—then followed up by providing everyone with flashlights, since that is one of the most important items to have on hand for personal safety.

Professional and Job-Related Skills Training

Every Dasher employee receives training in the Dasher Way, the Entrepreneurial Operating System® (EOS®)[26,] Health Insurance Portability and Accountability Act (HIPAA) regulations and data security, and job-related technical, computer, business reading and writing, and relationship skills.

The Dasher Way and EOS®

Dasher's initial training focuses on the Dasher Way (presented in Chapter 3). New employees learn about Dasher's culture during their orientation and through videos presented by senior leadership describing Dasher's values and behaviors and the importance that we place on their adherence. They each receive a brochure that lists, classifies by value, and describes each behavior. Their knowledge is cemented by weekly videos and Stand-Up Meeting discussions of the Dasher Way in which all employees take part. We also delve deeply with every employee into anti-harassment and anti-discrimination policies that are central to Dasher's value of being caring and respectful.

New employees learn in general terms about the system Dasher uses to run the company, EOS®, during orientation. (EOS® is explained in Chapter 7.) Their supervisor provides transparency in expectations, goals, and priorities for our team, including how they are established, monitored, and evaluated.

In addition, all employees receive regular training on the tools and processes of EOS®. The result of initial and ongoing education about our operating system is predictability, which is one of the major sources of trust in our workforce. The deep understanding Dasher provides to employees at all levels of EOS® not only reduces surprises and misunderstanding but also fosters team member participation in setting their own goals and measuring progress.

HIPAA and Data Security

Dasher provides HIPAA training to all employees who work in our office regardless of their position, which exceeds what is required by regulation. This eliminates any chance that someone lacking this knowledge will be handling or even in a position to view protected or sensitive information. As required for regulatory compliance, Dasher also delivers Medicare fraud, waste, and abuse training.

Dasher's well-developed, sophisticated data security measures are a source of competitive advantage and a reason that clients are able to trust Dasher. That is why we invest time up front with new employees and also on a continuing basis in data security training. We also show them how to apply the same types of precautions to keep their computers and mobile devices safe at home.

Specific Job-Related Skills

Dasher provides technical training customized to the job expectations of each role. For most staff, we offer basic computer skills through online seminars, as well as one-on-one tutoring and group live training on widely-used software such Excel and Outlook.

Dasher team members often have deficits in business writing and reading comprehension. We provide training, as well as one-on-one coaching in both areas.

Our menu of training opportunities includes conflict

management, a skill that is also often lacking in low-wage economically fragile employees. Our leaders have noticed this void and the role it plays in elevating the level of stress our team members experience because they lack ways to de-escalate situations both at work and at home. Our team members welcome strengthened skills in relationship management, assertiveness, and conflict resolution because of their applicability to much of their life outside of Dasher.

We regularly provide highly specialized education to Dasher's professional team of community healthcare workers. This includes timely, leading-edge training on motivational interviewing, health- and condition-related topics such as lactation, and trauma-informed care.

For example, Dasher provided the means, in terms of financial assistance, work flexibility, and emotional support, for a staff member to obtain certification as an Emergency Medical Technician when she expressed her desire to elevate her skills to this level. Another of our teammates with a newfound passion for SharePoint requested training, and Dasher is providing it.

All new employees receive one-on-one process training, or job shadowing and ride-along opportunities, or both. That may mean accompanying one of our people who work out in the field, driving from point-to-point to do their job, or sitting down next to another employee at their desk and walking through the steps of a process to enable the learner to create a checklist or other training tool for themselves. All of Dasher's key processes are documented to facilitate learning the end-to-end operation of a particular service even when our employee is responsible for only a portion of it.

If you are an employer, you may be asking, "Why invest all this money in people if they're going to leave their jobs, if there's going to be turnover?" What we are essentially trying to do is equip our low-wage, economically fragile workers with the skills that they need to become economically stable. That actually makes them good employees for anyone, not just Dasher. Now you are wondering, "Why train someone to be a good employee for somebody else?" Our answer is that some people will move on to better opportunities, and we wish them well. But most people want to stay. Because when someone is investing in you in a way that makes you feel valued and feel like you can be yourself, you are not going anywhere.

If you focus on your people—what they want, how they think, and what matters to them—you will not have to worry about turnover.

Our patience with learning styles and our focus on providing extensive training positions Dasher well to execute the next step in the *Team Member Prosperity and Success Model*, Leadership.

Voices of Dasher

Sofia, a community healthcare worker, has been with Dasher for three years. She learned about Dasher when she was working as a recruiter and felt called to apply. Dasher supported her in pursuing her goal of becoming certified as an EMT. She says her friends and her husband get jealous, seeing how happy she is in her job.

Sofia says:

This job was something that I felt pretty called to do. I really love my job. I love what I do here. I've never worked for a company that has done this much good for me and I feel like we're doing great in the community, too.

The things we do here, and the values—it's really good stuff. I feel good about coming to work every day. . . .

I was looking for some way that I could continue this job but add some skills to it. I thought that having some medical training would help when I'm speaking to members of the community as a healthcare worker, and Dasher gave me full support in every sense of the word. It was really hard for me at 51 years old, going back to school, doing school work, and working full time for six months.

There were times when I got a little frustrated and thought, "I don't know if I'm going to be able to finish this," but I did it. I passed the national certification, the written and hands-on portion. It was definitely great.

It's almost like it's a family here, the way we're treated. Our opinions matter. . . . I feel like a valued employee. I feel like we're valued here, for who we are and what we do.

What has Dasher done for me? If I could sum up, it's given me a job that I'm passionate about and that I continue to be passionate about. I'm also growing in it. Now that we've expanded I'm doing new projects, which is really cool. It's helping me and the community lead a healthy and happy lifestyle.

Chapter 7

The Dasher Model: Leadership

STEP FOUR of the *Team Member Prosperity and Success Model* is Leadership. This step could be more aptly named, Servant Leadership. To quote leadership expert John Maxwell, "leadership is influence."[27] Dasher's influence comes from enabling the success of others through transparency, predictability, and consistency in how we lead.

Our executive leadership team is aligned around all aspects of the *Team Member Prosperity and Success Model*. We are consistent in our delivery methods and message content for setting and communicating goals and expectations, for coaching and developing for teammates, for evaluating performance, and for rewarding positive behaviors and strong results.

Dasher's leadership processes are heavily indebted to the EOS®, which provides the basis for consistency, transparency, and predictability. It is the means by which we align all the aspects of our business to produce the results we identify. We have read every book by EOS® creator Gino Wickman.

The way our leaders implement EOS™, with compassion, humility, and eagerness to build mutual trust, is what tailors the process to low-income, economically fragile employees and distinguishes the way Dasher leads from most other organizations.

The leadership process starts with setting very clear expectations for Dasher as a company and derivatively for each employee so that they have a solid understanding of their role and how they fit into the company.

Dasher has an Accountability Chart™ (not an organizational chart) that shows every role and the key duties of that role in the organization. Dasher leaders present the chart to all employees, both for understanding and for their feedback in shaping the employee's role.

Each employee performing a role in the Accountability Chart™ is accountable for the metrics on a scorecard that fits their role and for completion of goals that they work out each quarter with their manager.

Prescribed, regular, verbal communication is central to providing the professional support and hands-on leadership that enables people with low self-assurance, more limited education and job-relevant experience, and a traumatic personal history to thrive. The personal nature of these interactions and the frequency with which they take place dramatically increase the odds that team members will understand what is expected and succeed in meeting expectations. The trust that is built through this process is inherent to its success.

Dasher teammates have daily interaction with their supervisor that is choreographed to ensure its effectiveness. A lower employee-to-supervisor ratio is essential to sustain the intensity of interaction; for example, the employee-to-supervisor ratio at Dasher is typically 7:1. You may ask, "How can you afford that?" Our answer is that this model pays for itself in lower risk of missed goals, higher productivity, and improved employee retention. The performance of Dasher's service level delivery to clients demonstrates that intense leadership results in more outbound calls made, more inbound calls answered, fewer escalated calls, more caller concerns handled first time final, more interactions that are positive and meaningful to callers, and fewer caller complaints.

Recognizing that Dasher is an organization working with people who, because of their background or previous experiences, may benefit from more feedback and reassurance than most employers are accustomed to providing, we do not leave regular communication to chance. It occurs daily, weekly, quarterly, and annually and is focused on two-way communication. In fact, supervisors are coached to listen more than talk to assure that employees are able to express what is important and that they feel heard, understood, and valued.

Daily Communication

The supervisors' day starts with Dasher's Huddle, a 15-minute meeting that sets the stage for the day. Each Dasher leader in turn communicates face-to-face any key information (we term this the Headlines), their goals for the day's accomplishments (which we call the Weather), and any obstacles they anticipate or know of that will hinder their success (known at Dasher as Traffic). Resources can be redirected, problems solved, and priorities shifted in the moment.

Daily Huddle is followed by a similar quick huddle at cascading levels. Each person receives an individual check-in with their leader as well. While it can be phone, text, email, or in person, our team stresses the value of voice and in-person connections because that is how the richest communication occurs and trusting relationships are built.

In addition, leaders learn to have frequent ad hoc quick conversations for in-the-moment teaching and mentoring. If somebody is not doing something that they need to be doing, that conversation happens right away, and it is always one-on-one. Dasher leaders take care that no negative feedback is ever given other than in a one-on-one setting and that all feedback is delivered with an eye on maintaining the dignity of both parties.

Weekly Communication

Every week, we have a "Stand-Up" Meeting for the entire Dasher team. There are no chairs. With our encouragement, what is said runs the gamut. Our leadership team models the free sharing of updates and headlines about key clients and projects. Some people talk about the fact that their kids made a touchdown in football last week. Somebody else talks about the fact that they achieved a

100 percent quality score. Yet another might have a request for the group: "I am going to be out next week with surgery and I would appreciate all the good thoughts."

All of this communication is supported by Dasher TV, a video monitor with a looping reel delivering messages about the Dasher Way and photos showing events in the team's personal lives, and important company information.

Each department, starting with the executive leadership team, has a weekly team problem-solving meeting. Every employee participates in the one for their department. They will spend 30 to 90 minutes identifying problems and issues that they and their colleagues are having in meeting the expectations that Dasher has for our company and for delivering exceptional service to clients.

Issues that are identified and later solved might be meeting a customer's particular need, or figuring out a work schedule that is fair to everybody while delivering on Dasher's service level agreements, or issues with sourcing—anything that affects Dasher, our clients, or our employees is fair game. The team works together in this small-group setting to prioritize issues and then find solutions together.

In these weekly team meetings there is also communication about how the department is doing—whether or not scorecard metrics are on track, and how their key priorities are going. Frequently reviewing and discussing metrics naturally leads to the identification of barriers, problems, and concerns.

In addition to a weekly meeting as a group, each employee has a weekly one-on-one check-in meeting with their manager to exchange information and feedback. It may take only 10 minutes, or it can take an hour. However long it takes, each employee knows they have uninterrupted private time with their manager to talk about whatever is on their mind.

The weekly one-on-one meeting is another way of showing respect for people—their dignity and their value.

Quarterly Communication

Dasher Quarterly Conversations are a time for the manager and the employee to deepen and strengthen their relationship. Leaders are coached to use specific open-ended conversation starter questions to get people talking and to listen generously to any response. A manager will ask, "What is going well for you?" and probe the response, asking more questions to understand what the employee is saying. With each question—"What is not going well for you? If you could change something, what would you change?"—leaders learn to dig for understanding of what the employee is saying and what it means to him or her.

There is great satisfaction on the part of team members when they feel truly heard. These sessions create psychological safety in addition to building trust. This is especially true of people who have experienced how it feels to not be heard or respected at work.

Annual Communication

Annually, each employee and manager meet in person to discuss the performance of the employee in the previous year. The annual discussion is the culmination of all of the daily, weekly, and quarterly discussions that have occurred and therefore rarely contains any surprises.

Its focus is on how the employee lives the Dasher Way, how well the employee understands their job, how passionate they are about doing the job, and how well they perform it. It is one page that summarizes for discussion the bare essentials of what is important. There is no rating besides "yes or no" on each element of the nine-item appraisal, so it is easy to understand and to use to focus on what, if anything, needs to change.

Rewards/Gotcha!

Dasher leaders are expected to catch people doing things right. Frequent positive feedback is essential to guide, reassure, and inspire.

Dasher has an internally-developed rewards program called the Gotcha Program that provides quick recognition when an employee is on the right track. Whenever any employee observes a behavior that constitutes one of the Dasher Way behaviors—when they see the Dasher Way in action—they can nominate another employee to receive points that are equivalent to cash.

For example, when an employee experiences or observes someone being caring and respectful, such as helping a teammate with some aspect of their job without it being required, that employee can nominate their teammate for a Gotcha award.

Each nomination is reviewed—we have a specific process for that—and then points are assigned. Over time our employees accumulate Gotcha points, which they can cash in any time they want to do so. This is quick positive feedback and it is meaningful to people. For instance, if today they get a Gotcha nomination and they are awarded 20 points, then tomorrow or even later today, the awardee can request that $20 and get it right away.

One of our teammates with 100 accumulated Gotcha points needed her clothes washer repaired. She submitted a voucher and said, "I am cashing in my Gotcha points." Within a few minutes, we handed her $100.

Dasher makes it possible to donate Gotcha points to a fellow employee's account—and this happens! One of our teammates collected Gotcha dollars and used the money to purchase gift cards which he gifted anonymously to two of his colleagues.

A large benefit of Gotcha is that it has people continually looking for examples of behaviors that constitute the Dasher Way, watching for someone doing something special for a client, like handling someone on the phone with great care, or suppressing their own frustrations to be sympathetic to a caller or a client or another employee.

Course Correction

Dasher has high expectations for its employees. We have a three-step course correction process. Each one of three steps is a face-to-face conversation with the employee to talk about specifically which values they are deviating from or how they might be showing an inability to understand their job, do their job, and want their job.

Dasher leaders are trained to be very specific about deviations from expectations, and they are prepared with multiple examples. They are also coached to deliver the feedback in a way that preserves the dignity of all parties. Leaders do not talk down to people. Conversations on any topic are adult-to-adult.

The substance of each discussion is what each person—the employee and the manager—will do to get back on track. Just as the employee must commit to concrete steps that he or she believes will eliminate the deviation from expectations, so, too, the supervisor makes a commitment: training, more coaching, behavior modeling, perhaps role playing.

After the first course correction meeting, there will be another sit-down 30 days later. The manager evaluates the same issue, and, if everything is on track, that is the end of it. If it is not, the steps repeat and lead up to a third discussion.

If the situation has not improved as needed, which happens rarely, chances are that there is not a fit for the employee at Dasher. The severance process proceeds with dignity and respect, consistent with Dasher's values.

The steps in Dasher's course correction process are explained to all employees as part of their orientation. Supervisors are trained on implementation of the course correction process, including role play. This makes it predictable, consistent, and free of surprises, all of which are requirements for Dasher to be considered a trustworthy organization by a group of people who have not always felt their encounters with authority were supportive, fair, or respectful.

Well before the course correction process comes into play, Dasher provides a comprehensive support system, described in the next chapter, which makes course correction a last resort.

Voices of Dasher

Jessica is an outbound call representative and community healthcare worker. In her three years at Dasher, she has faced multiple difficulties in her personal life—a ceiling collapse that destroyed the beds in her home, a persistent, mysterious malfunction in her car, a serious car accident—but with Dasher's help, she has kept moving forward in spite of it all.

Jessica says:

Dasher has been very helpful. It's my family away from home. . . .

I think our values are amazing here. It's the values and the teamwork. The values are something I think everybody should live on a day-to-day basis. . . .

Gotchas are our reward from our coworkers, our supervisors, anybody who catches anybody doing something good, living the Dasher Way with Dasher values. I got one just the other day from a coworker. I wasn't expecting to be rewarded for bringing in exercise equipment—I figure if I have equipment and people want to use it, I'm going to bring it in. That's just who I am. I was rewarded cash for just being me—it's kind of cool that you can be rewarded for just being me.

I got one when I face painted at the company picnic. I like drawing and painting; I'm very creative. They wanted me to face paint, so I painted and I enjoyed it and I came into work and I had Gotcha bucks!

Chapter 8

The Dasher Model: Support Systems

SUPPORT SYSTEMS ARE an integral part of Dasher's *Team Member Prosperity and Success Model*. From our experience, support systems are vitally important for companies that have a low-wage, economically fragile workforce.

Low-wage, economically fragile people are more likely to lack the time, money, experience, social capital, and networks to enable them to prevent life's crises. They often have greater exposure to trauma as children, and research now shows[28] that high exposure to childhood trauma and behaviors contrary to success at work are highly correlated.

Employer Impact

Gallup's *State of the American Workplace* report made employee disengagement a highly visible workforce issue. What's even more important is that Gallup gave business leaders a method for estimating the cost of employee engagement based on a cost of $3,400 for every $10,000 in salary.[29]

It seems like common sense to us that employees who are anxious about their children, food, housing, transportation, or health have less capacity to meet or exceed Dasher's expectations for quality and productivity. Under these circumstances, it's simply not possible to be an engaged employee even when you want to be one.

Poor service has the same impact on a business that termites have on a house. To understand what this means to Dasher, consider our call center, which helps people facing situations that are anxiety-producing and stressful. It is up to Dasher call center representatives to reassure them, to provide them with information, and to help them to accomplish their objectives. If Dasher employees are also highly stressed from the conditions of their own personal lives, they will be less skilled and less attentive in delivering caring, helpful, and resourceful service.

Employee Impact

Dasher's service delivery capabilities require us to have a focused, present workforce. For this reason and others, Dasher provides all of its employees with respectful, dignified, decision-making support as well as resources (flexible work time, knowledge of alternative ways to handle problems, emotional support, and, when needed, money).

Though we focus on economically fragile people in describing the *Team Member Prosperity and Success Model*, we apply the process to everyone at Dasher. We are all susceptible to stressors that reduce the quality of our decision-making and the pressure does not have to come from economic fragility. For example, a recent *Time* magazine profile of renowned tennis professional, Serena Williams, described the worst loss of her tennis career.[30] Ten minutes before the start of the tennis match, Serena learned that the man who had been incarcerated for murdering her older sister had just been paroled. If anyone knows about performing under pressure, it is Serena Williams, but she simply could not play well under the stress of such emotionally devastating information.

Similarly, when low-wage, economically fragile people are faced with a crisis, decision-making is impaired. Long-term concerns get pushed to the periphery. For example, an employee who is preoccupied with paying for food or having to fix their only car might succumb to a high interest loan or withdrawal of 401K savings.

At Dasher, we have many examples of how economically fragile people make less than optimal decisions while under pressure.

Unfortunately, poor decision-making typically opens the door for victimization by unscrupulous service providers. Services include short-term, very high interest loans, check cashing, bill payment, tax preparation and refund loans, and rent-to-own products. These services have the net effect of reducing the income of low-wage workers, making them less financially stable and more fragile by taking an outsized share of their earnings and depleting scarce resources needed for necessities.

Trauma-Informed Leadership

Recent research has offered some staggering statistics about the number of people who have significant trauma in their backgrounds. A joint CDC/Kaiser Permanente survey[31] studied the correlation between trauma, stress, and maltreatment in childhood, and health and wellbeing later in life. In this Adverse Childhood Experiences (ACEs) study, almost two-thirds of the participants—men and women—reported at least one childhood experience of physical or sexual abuse, neglect, or family dysfunction.

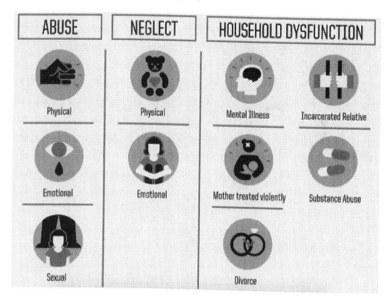

More than one in five reported three or more such experiences. These experiences were found to be highly correlated with worker performance problems, as well as serious emotional problems, health risk behaviors, social problems, adult disease and disability, mortality, and high health care and other costs.

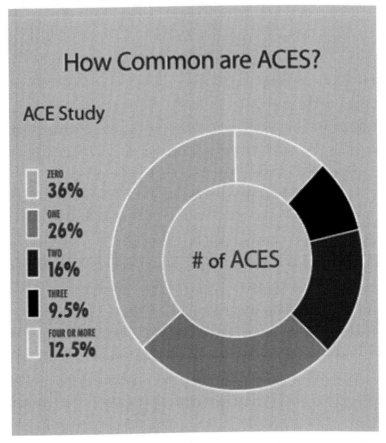

It is important to keep the impact of trauma in mind because it shows up again and again in a variety of circumstances and can be an obstacle to development.

Trauma is a combination of the body and the mind's way of handling the rush of feelings and thoughts that might follow a painful or terrifying experience like a job loss, a car accident, public ridicule, or living in a dysfunctional family. The concentration of thoughts and feelings from traumatic experiences reside within us. They stay there for years, maybe for a lifetime. Sometimes we are conscious of them and sometimes not.

People develop coping skills to mask their trauma. Some people are better at it than others. We can see trauma manifesting, for example, in people with low self-confidence—maybe they are so shy they cannot make eye contact. They may have low self-esteem, depression, and anxiety, and these mental states may come and go in and out of their life. On a Friday they are fine and then on Monday they are depressed.

Dasher Leaders Expect to Help

Whether it is help in making decisions, deflecting financial scams, working with the symptoms of childhood trauma, or providing support when resources are depleted, Dasher leaders are sensitized, educated, and expected to recognize the need and to meet it. They embrace their role as trauma-informed leaders, which is to make team members feel cared for in every interaction.

The fundamental core of trauma-informed approaches is to change the question from "What is wrong with this person?" to "What happened to this person that they are reacting to this situation in the way that they are?" Then we ask ourselves how we can adapt the situation.

For instance, when someone who suffered abuse in an educational setting reacts poorly to classroom training and a test at the end, we look for a different way to help them acquire the knowledge they need. Having that knowledge is not negotiable, but how the knowledge gets delivered is.

Dasher Employee Assistance Fund

Aware that economically fragile employees simply have more catastrophes with an economic impact due to the lack of a personal safety net, Dasher has created an employee assistance fund to help meet those needs.

The employee assistance fund is fully funded by contributions from Dasher and from our executives. Typically, a grant from the fund makes it possible for our teammates to continue working. Without granting money, we would lose a great teammate, have to recruit, hire, and train another employee, and manage the morale issues associated with existing employees having larger workloads until the new person is fully functional.

In one instance, an employee was evicted from her apartment because of flooding from the apartment above hers. The flooding damaged her possessions, and she was ordered to vacate because the damage to her apartment was not going to be repaired. She did not have the protection of a lease or the money to pay a security deposit on another apartment, making homelessness the most likely outcome. Through the Dasher employee assistance fund, she received a non-taxable grant to pay her security deposit and the cost of a U-Haul for moving to new stable housing.

The Dasher employee assistance fund helped another employee pay her water bill when her service was about to be turned off for nonpayment. Because her quarterly bill had increased unexpectedly and precipitously, she did not have the money to pay it. A grant paid the bill to be paid and then also paid for a plumber to diagnose what had happened so she could prevent it from happening again. She is now on stable ground.

Another employee went home to find an eviction notice on her apartment door. Her significant other, who had assumed responsibility to pay the rent, failed to do so, and instead cleaned out their bank account and left town, abandoning her and their children. Dasher paid the rent and the cost of changing the locks because she feared this individual.

Another employee, for whom public transportation was not an option, was driving a car that quit without warning when she was driving to work. Dasher helped her find a trustworthy garage that was able to diagnose the problem. Dasher negotiated a loaner car for her and took her to the garage to pick it up. The Dasher emergency fund paid the cost to repair the car.

Voices of Dasher

Shondra, an outbound call center representative, has been with Dasher for almost two years. Not long ago her husband got sick and had to stop working. The loss of his income meant that they fell behind on their rent. With the help of a grant from Dasher's employee assistance fund, Shondra's family was able to weather the crisis. Since then Shondra has been participating in the SmartDollar program at Dasher, working toward a more stable financial future.

Shondra says:

I was stressing out for weeks. They really helped me out. I don't know what my husband and I would've done if they hadn't helped us. We were facing eviction. With him not working it's a big burden on me to try to carry the load by myself. Miss Cyndi and Dasher were a godsend. They made sure I got what I needed. I am very grateful for that and the people at Dasher—the way that we're treated like family. They're a work family. . . .

They're always encouraging us to better ourselves, and coming to work is such a pleasure. Most call center jobs are rigid and people there don't speak to each other. Here you really feel everyone and their situation. If they're going through something—good, bad, or indifferent—it doesn't matter. I feel like everybody can talk to each other in the office. And the values are good. . . .

You want everyone to treat each other nicely when you're at work. Here it almost feels like euphoria at work. Since we're a smaller office, you feel that connection. I think it gives us an opportunity to really know each other and care about each other.

I feel really blessed to be in this position. I think everything we do here is positive. It's directed toward helping all of us be better people.

Support for Wellness

Support for Dasher employees' health and wellness is also an integral part of the *Team Member Prosperity and Success Model*. Some of our employees suffer from food insecurity, so we regularly make groceries available, along with breakfasts, healthy snacks, and lunches—often in conjunction with our educational sessions.

In another situation, a Dasher employee needed a liver transplant. On the transplant list awaiting an available organ, he reached a point where he was no longer able to work. Dasher continued to pay its company contribution to offset his COBRA enabling him to maintain group health insurance, even after his medical leave and his employment with us ended. Without health insurance, the transplant would not have been possible, and he would have died. Following a successful transplant, thanks to the continuation of his insurance, he has returned to work part-time. His wife now works for Dasher as well.

Sometimes Dasher support comes in the form of helping to facilitate healthier living. For instance, two of our employees wanted to quit smoking. Because the cost of nicotine patches was prohibitive, Dasher paid for them. The entire team encouraged them in their quest to stop smoking, just as they do employees who are trying to lose weight or become more fit.

Sometimes Dasher support comes in the form of being there for a team member who does not have a family to help in times of difficulty. An employee required outpatient surgery, which she faced alone. On the day of her operation, senior leaders texted with her frequently to reassure her, to boost her confidence, and to let her know that we were closely monitoring her situation. She gave Dasher's president her hospital patient identification number so that we could continuously track her progress through the surgical process.

When our teammate was discharged, she received a delivery of groceries at her home. It was an easier day and perhaps a better outcome because she knew she was not alone.

Support for Whatever Comes Up

When members of the team have issues with the quality of their housing, Dasher is there to assist them in resolving them. There are landlords who refuse to make necessary repairs, unfairly withhold security deposits, and charge for utilities or costs incurred by a prior tenant.

We made it easy for an employee to help her mother in Puerto Rico in the aftermath of Hurricane Maria by being flexible in approving remote work and personal time off.

We found a dental provider and provided transportation when a teammate without a car required multiple dental procedures to mitigate extreme pain.

We introduce teammates to Pennsylvania's Health Insurance Premium Payment Program (HIPP) and help them to enroll in this program, which covers deductibles and co-pays for health insurance.

One of our teammates rented an apartment that had no heat in the middle of winter. The landlord was very slow to repair the problem. Dasher provided her with heaters and blankets.

Support to Thrive

These are just a few examples of support for employees, which pays dividends to Dasher in terms of retaining our employees and increasing their effectiveness at work.

Being caring and respectful is the Dasher Way. The assistance provided aligns with our mission to help people to live happy, healthy lives.

It is also more cost effective to provide this support than to go through the process of recruiting, hiring, and training new employees. This reality comes into greater focus in the next chapter on personal and professional development.

Chapter 9

The Dasher Model:

Personal and Professional Development

THE LAST TWO COMPONENTS of our *Team Member Prosperity and Success Model* are personal and professional development. Both are intertwined, and many of the elements we have discussed in the previous chapters contribute to them.

People develop skills incrementally, and in our experience, professional growth happens at about the same pace as personal growth among low-wage, economically fragile workers. As we get further along in professional development, we may uncover issues that we did not realize existed. For example, we commonly find that reading comprehension and grammar are weak. Self-expression is also a critical skill that is often missing.

Counterintuitive Education

We encourage people to grow through quarterly education presentations that we offer on company time. Often, we provide a meal at the session, as well as attractive giveaways; we create a fun atmosphere that does not even remotely resemble a classroom. Our presentations cover topics such as data security, computer skills, career-related skills, personal safety, and wellness.

In 2007, the Urban Institute published a study titled *Innovative Employment Approaches and Programs for Low-Income Families.*[32] Even though this study is more than a decade old, its findings echo our own experience at Dasher. While the study did not offer specific recommendations, it did conclude that the combination of personal and professional development is effective.

We took this concept a step further and started mixing up seemingly unrelated topics and linking them together. We just tried it, and it worked. Why? Because everybody is at a different spot on their journey, and everybody is ready to receive a different message at different times. For example, we combined a personal finance topic with a presentation on how to have more energy. It was a big hit.

Trauma

In Chapter 8, Support Systems, we referred to Adverse Childhood Experiences and the broad impact of trauma on our workforce. In personal and professional development, trauma shows up again and again. That is a sobering part of this work. It might seem like a roadblock, but it does not have to be. We have come to believe that the work environment can be actually the right setting for employees experiencing trauma. Some might say that sounds crazy, but people need to believe that they deserve positive change. They need to be guided to slowly develop skills in which they can see their own progress and then connect that progress with making change occur in their lives generally. And they need to experience the personal success that builds confidence to take on risks and new tasks that are appropriately challenging. Recently, we introduced a slogan about how we often wait until we are not afraid to do something. We now encourage each other to "do it afraid."

The workplace is actually a great setting to move people from being economically fragile to economically stable.

Mindset

At Dasher, we were inspired by a book titled, *Mindset: The New Psychology of Success*, by Carol Dweck. In her book, Dr. Dweck explains two different types of mindset. One is a fixed mindset, and the other is a growth mindset.[33]

People with a fixed mindset believe that qualities are inborn and fixed. We either have them or we do not. People with a growth mindset believe that abilities can be developed and strengthened through commitment, hard work, and effort.

Why is this important? There are business leaders who have a fixed mindset. They have already decided that low-wage, economically fragile workers cannot learn. They believe the capabilities of low- wage, economically fragile workers are set in stone. That fixed mindset, where it exists, deeply affects one's ability to help people grow.

One of Dasher's core values is Able to Learn. We are believers in the growth mindset. Why? Because as we say all the time, Dasher is us. Dasher, the organization, can meet higher expectations when the people at Dasher can meet higher expectations.

Because we are focused on attracting and engaging with low-wage, economically fragile workers, and because we have an emphasis on helping them become economically stable, we look for jobs and projects that present opportunities for professional and personal growth. Many of these projects are in interpersonal communication—inbound calls, outbound calls, field staff—and the expectations on our staff get raised in a lot of these projects.

For example, Dasher is preparing to kick off a call center project that is going to take calls about auto emissions. Now we have teammates who have learned and can understand the auto emissions business, as well as how to be a call center representative.

We have a large-scale project that involves assembling 68,000 information packets. Each information packet is a folder with eight different pieces in it and there are 20 versions of the packet. Managing the materials, the orders, and the timeframe for that is a challenge which gives people a chance to step up and grow.

We are preparing to deploy field staff to go work in an emergency department and talk to people about their asthma. Now we have people who have learned to communicate face-to-face and talk about asthma.

We have always had a consistent focus on data security, but now Dasher is going to be certified with a much higher level of data security, called Service Organization Control Type 2 (SOC 2). It is a third-party evaluation that entails an external organization evaluating our data security procedures and policies, and certifying that Dasher is actually secure. We have had to educate our teammates and implement stringent policies and procedures. It is another part of the development process, because we started out training employees on the basics of data security, which we still do, but now we have built on that with the SOC 2.

For example, one of the things we do for various clients is develop databases specifically for collecting information that we can gather through inbound phone calls or outbound phone calls and deploying field staff. The people who come to work for us do learn about the importance and meaning of data. Being able to measure the results of our work is really critical.

Another learning opportunity Dasher provides is our tracking of how many lives we have impacted positively. We came up with the idea of measuring the number of constructive interactions that we have with people. We defined a constructive interaction as some interpersonal communication with a client's constituent that transfers information of value to that constituent. We actually track how many constructive interactions we have, and we look for projects that allow us to increase the number of constructive interactions. That puts our team in a position to deliver value. It is part of our ongoing development not only as individuals but also as an organization.

Many organizations take the completion of a task to be the end of their responsibility, but at Dasher we want the task to have had a measurable impact. We want our clients to know that we have actually accomplished something for them. This is a way of thinking that we help our low-wage, economically fragile workers to understand, and it extends back into their own lives because they realize the value of taking an action that actually accomplishes something. It is those actions that are important.

To ensure the continued success of our business, we have to continually raise the sophistication of Dasher. Because Dasher is all of us, we have to continually raise the sophistication level of our team.

This is the growth mindset. It really is possible to help people get there if there is a systematic process in place that provides all the elements of support they need. The world moves. Expectations change all the time. As a company, Dasher is always looking to increase its capabilities and meet higher expectations.

Personal Development Focus

Dasher's personal development emphasizes personal well-being, kindness, and self-care. With so much diversity in our workforce, we have a wonderful mixture of cultures and belief systems that add richness, variety, and complexity. We encourage all of our employees to grow in ways that matter to them. We stress to employees that if they are growing personally, they can develop much more professionally. Personal development is their platform for professional development. For example, we have teammates who have decided to quit smoking—with our support and encouragement—embracing Dasher's commitment to healthier living. Achieving such a difficult personal goal encourages people to reach for professional goals, as well.

Professional Development Focus

In business, we want positive, measurable results. But here we need to focus almost exclusively on praising effort. We want our employees to understand that their effort can result in their growth, and their growth can lead to economic stability.

We praise the effort that they put into growing those skills, and we praise their skill level to eliminate or alleviate fear and doubt. If we tell someone, "Hey, you are brilliant," or "You are awesome," we may think we are doing a good thing when in fact we are not. It is counter-productive because we are setting a standard for that person. They become concerned that they will not be able to maintain that standard and fear that they can only go down from there. They end up avoiding growth opportunities—they want to avoid having their manager come back and say they are no longer brilliant. For professional development, we focus on the effort.

Mentoring

Traditional mentoring is helping employees understand the best way to move forward in their careers. For example, someone in the banking industry can mentor someone in the insurance industry regarding how to advance in their field. Mentoring low-wage, economically fragile workers does not work the same way.

Dasher's mentoring relationships are non-traditional. Our senior executives mentor low-wage, economically fragile workers by building a trusting relationship and establishing a mutual understanding that the mentor is there to help the mentee accomplish their personal goals. Dasher is helping people understand the best way to move forward toward an economically stable life. This is a special set of discussions.

Dasher mentoring is role modeling, helping teach new skills, and boosting confidence. Mentors on our team understand the social behaviors of teammates and use that understanding to help with personal development. It is important to focus on the individual's specific challenge and how this challenge may relate to childhood trauma. It is an ongoing conversation—often incorporated into our Quarterly Conversations—and it has to feel comfortable, that is, noninvasive, non-intimidating, and non-threatening.

Some of the areas where we see the need for personal development are self-expression, listening, comprehension, conflict management, and basic writing skills. Of course, these also cross over into professional development.

Through mentoring, we look for ways to help our teammates move toward a growth mindset. For example, we have an employee we think has the potential to eventually become a supervisor. She had a fear—a fixed mindset—about conflict. She told us, "I do not do conflict well. I do not want to be involved in conflict. I just want to sit at my desk and do my job, and I do not want to have any conflict with anybody."

We could have simply passed over her for a promotion or forced her into the role with negative consequences to follow. Instead, we invited her to join us for a conflict management workshop. It offered techniques and tips about conflict, how to defuse it, de-escalate it, and make it less scary. She was intrigued by the workshop and now has more confidence in her ability. At the same time, her mentor was on hand to clarify and help reinforce lessons taught in the session that included jargon she did not easily comprehend.

This training and the mentoring she is receiving are moving her toward economic stability because she has more of a path to promotion. Again, it is both personal and professional development.

Dream Management

This may seem like an odd topic for a business model. We are committed to providing equal access to prosperity for all in the way they define it. We believe in the premise of Matthew Kelly's book *The Dream Manager*, "a business parable about how companies can achieve remarkable results by helping their employees fulfill their dreams."[34]

We know that happy, healthy people have hopes and dreams for the future, so part of our focus in the *Team Member Prosperity and Success Model* is helping our team members make their dreams attainable.

Employees stay in jobs when they feel their job is helping them move toward a better future. That does not mean that they need a meteoric rise up the corporate ladder. They want to know what might be in store for them if they stay employed in the same place.

Some organizations pay for college or other educational opportunities, which is great. Among low-wage, economically fragile workers, there are other dreams—like learning to speak better English, learning to be economically literate, securing special training for a child, becoming an emergency medical technician, getting a new car, having beds in every room, or even having the right dishes. Their dreams are not extravagant, but they are very important.

Dream management can sometimes blend into crisis management, and we are in the process of helping people dealing with a variety of economic challenges to understand the difference. When we work on dream management with a Dasher teammate, the first step is understanding where they want to head and what their objectives are. We recognize that all of these objectives are really important to them, and we help them see a path to getting there.

For example, Dasher hired an employee who did not have a high school diploma or a GED, because we recognized her aligned values and evident passion. Her dream was to go to college and become a certified Christian counselor, but she had not completed high school. Dasher provided incentives and support for her to obtain a high school equivalency diploma (GED®). This included access to tutoring and constant encouragement. She successfully passed the GED®. Now enrolled in college courses, she continues to receive Dasher encouragement and tutoring and believes that her dream of becoming a Christian counselor is finally within her grasp. You will read her story in *Voices of Dasher*, which follows.

Our teammate says that it was only because of the encouragement the Dasher team provided and our belief in her that she finally has cleared the obstacles to the future she envisions for herself.

Another employee is passionate about archeology and history. She found a once-in-a-lifetime opportunity to be part of an archeological dig in our local area. The problem was that the dig took place during normal business hours. Encouraged by Dasher to design her own work schedule around the dig, she, too, realized her dream.

Voices of Dasher

Gail is a customer service representative. When she joined Dasher two years ago, she had been trying off and on for years to get her GED. It was a condition of her employment that she complete her GED within a year. Not only did she achieve that goal, she went on to enroll in college, where she is studying psychology and pursuing her long-time dream of becoming a Christian counselor.

Gail says:

When I first started here I was already taking night classes, so that built up my confidence. There was fear that I would not finish, but the people around me were confident and positive and kind of brought that out in me. I'm still pushing towards my confidence and my boldness but it helps when you surround yourself with that atmosphere. . . .

The confidence that I started building led me to other areas outside of Dasher in my own personal life. We have a Refit class here once a week. We get together, we have fun, and we do what we do trying to work out. When you're smoking and not eating healthy, that is kind of hard to do. It made me want to get myself together.

This is amazing to me—where I came from and where I am. Just to know that I can do college, to know that I did get my GED at 50, to know that I can take classes, to do the things that I want—is amazing. The things that I used to want or imagine that I wanted, I now see myself getting. It wasn't always like that. I didn't always see myself. That's where it starts. You've got to see yourself there first, so you know you can achieve those things. I just have to thank everybody at Dasher because everybody has a part whether they admit it, whether they say it, or whether we speak it. I know for me, everybody has a position in how I'm forming my new way of life. So I want to thank everybody. We're family.

Chapter 10

Lessons Learned

WHEN WE STARTED OUT, we wanted to build a socially-driven company that was profitable enough to keep growing, where we could reinvest our profits into serving customers better and making the people who serve them prosperous.

We have come a long way, and we have arrived at a model that works, that we believe in and that we want to share.

Along the way, we have learned a great deal about what influences people and what does not. Here are some of the important lessons.

Trust is everything. Building trust with people is paramount before they can begin to believe. Economically fragile people have experienced numerous setbacks and many disappointments. They have learned to withhold trust. They will typically be less ready to trust compared to those whose life experiences have been more positive. At Dasher, we never stop working on building trust. We are also obsessively careful not to violate it, because trust lost is very hard to regain.

Everyone is different. Simply put, what works for one person is not guaranteed to work for another person. For example, being able to learn is one of Dasher's core values. That said, everybody has different learning styles. Adapting our approaches to training is a constant need.

Every behavior is rational. Even if we do not understand it and it appears unjustified, every behavior is rational. Most people from low-income backgrounds have suffered childhood trauma that impacts every aspect of their lives, including in the workplace. When we see a behavior that appears irrational, we look deeper to determine what is behind it. We are curious, open-minded, and ask useful questions.

The world is bigger than the workplace. People live in a much bigger world than just where they work. We have neither the undivided attention of our employees nor significant power over them. Family, friends, and the norms that define culture outside of work matter to and influence people. If we are trying to influence people and we are working against their family and friends and long-standing norms, it is going to be tough.

Well-understood shared values and behaviors are a must. Everybody needs to be on the same page. We believe this is the road map to success. We will serve our customers and each other well with these behaviors, and ultimately, we will be successful at work and at life with these behaviors. We hire and retain for cultural fit.

Behavior change takes time and requires patience. Personal and professional growth requires people to change. We have to give people room to be able to change their behavior. We cannot expect—just because we told them and they clearly heard us—that their behavior is going to change immediately. It takes the drip, drip, drip method of continually demonstrating the kinds of behaviors that are positive and lead to success. Patience is rewarded.

Listening is more important than talking. Having people freely talk about what is on their mind or what is getting in their way is considered a home run at Dasher. We need to know what we are doing that is working from the employee's vantage point. The real gold is in learning about what is not working for them.

Nobody gets it right the first time. We do not know what we do not know. That applies to us, as we design motivational exercises and training. Everything is iterative. Some of it has worked wonderfully. Some of it has not. We keep trying new things, and we start doing some things more effectively as we learn what sticks.

Tough enforcement of standards is essential. Our number one priority is to deliver a customer experience that makes working with Dasher attractive and productive. To do so requires strict adherence to standards. Being a compassionate, caring, welcoming, and empowering organization does not mean that we do not have standards or that we are softies. It just means that we strive to let people feel safe, supported, and understood in their quest to meet those standards.

Gossip is poison. We cannot allow gossip to exist, much less to flourish. By gossip, we mean discussing anything negative with someone who cannot help solve the problem. We talk about Dasher as a no-gossip zone. With a warning and a repeat, gossip is a firing offense because we know it is the kryptonite that can bring down our culture.

The most effective leadership is humble leadership. Humble leadership is listening with the intent to understand. It is innovation with the goal to make something better for our clients, our team, and our world. Humble leadership is saying, "Hey, we did not get that right this time. Let's try again." Humble leadership does not have all the answers—and knows it.

Being a values-oriented business is a competitive advantage. In this economy, with its focus on brands and messaging, every business must demonstrate value and separate itself from other businesses. By investing the time and money to attract and engage with low-wage, economically fragile people, Dasher is separating itself because we are truly different.

We are putting Dasher together with our customers on the same side of a very passionate issue. It is gratifying to see clients, prospects, prospective employees, and members of the community seek us out and want to be part of the solution.

You cannot outsource this. By now it should be obvious. This takes a top-down, organization-wide commitment to engaging with low-wage, economically fragile workers with the intent to help them become economically stable.

Go all in. This is not a program. It is not a project. It is not a manual. It is a way of being as an organization. It starts at the top and permeates the whole fabric of the organization. The Dasher model is not the only way. Other organizations can do this, and it will create more examples for others to follow.

<u>Keep learning and enjoy the process</u>. After 10 years, we are still learning and more importantly, we are still having fun. We listen to feedback, we understand it, we incorporate it, and we iterate, iterate, iterate—with a sense of great humility.

Chapter 11

The Dasher Challenge

IF YOU LEAD A BUSINESS, we hope that you will be inspired to provide the environment and support to your economically fragile workers to enable them to succeed in your company and move toward prosperity in their lives. Implementing a *Team Member Prosperity and Success Model* may seem daunting and have you wondering, "Where do I start?"

We did not do everything at once, and you don't have to either. You will begin to reap benefits in turnover, productivity, and quality if you make some key investments initially. The rest of the model can follow in stages.

How to Get Started

There are four things that we suggest you do first in order to launch an initiative to make your company a place where economically fragile workers can not only survive, but also thrive.

First, become educated regarding the Social Determinants of Health (SDOH) and Trauma-Informed Leadership practices and incorporate this awareness into your management training and human resources policy making. As noted in Chapter 2, SDOH are the social, cultural, political, economic, commercial, and environmental factors that shape the conditions in which people are born, grow, live, work, and age. These factors determine the health challenges that an individual is likely to face. Trauma-Informed Leadership, discussed in Chapter 8, takes into account the childhood experiences that lead people to be risk averse or blocked learners in situations that seem unsafe to them. The better you and your executive team understand why employees face challenges in attendance and at work, the more equipped you are to support them in ways that will improve attendance, productivity, and quality of work.

A second key step to launching a *Team Member Prosperity and Success Model* is to have someone on your staff, likely in human resources, who is trained and allowed ample time to devote to understanding and helping employees resolve problems like transportation, housing, parenting issues, etc., that may arise suddenly and make it difficult for them to get to work and focus on the job. As part of this effort, create a safe haven and encourage the use of SNAP and CHIP. Many times, those who are eligible will forgo these live-saving benefits to avoid the indignity of applying for them and using them.

Third, we suggest you direct some of the company's charitable dollars to establishing a fund exclusively for the purpose of granting money to employees in crisis. Your local community foundation can provide turnkey service in getting it set up. It can be the answer to unforeseen emergency expenses that will otherwise derail a good employee.

Fourth, you can do a food insecurity test. Purchase some commonly used grocery items at a popular grocery store. Commonly needed items are peanut butter, canned chicken and tuna, canned soup, canned fruits and vegetables, grain products and pasta, and macaroni and cheese mixes that require water instead of milk and butter.

Set them on a counter top where you might usually see donuts. Leave the grocery store bags there and write a note that says "help yourself." If the food disappears in a few days, you have food insecurity among your team.

What can you do if the test results are positive for food insecurity? It is not important to identify who is food insecure. There is no need to take over and solve this problem because your intervention can be viewed as interference. Consider a variety of options that can supplement food in the home. The people who need it also need a dignified way to get it. Provide healthy breakfast items and healthy snacks. Order extra pizza to ensure that there are leftovers. Have a supply of carryout containers for people to use. Raffle grocery store gift cards at company functions.

Once these are in place, you can assess where your next investment of support will have the greatest impact, whether it is in conflict management and wellness education or revamping your culture so your norms are clear and create a safe and supportive environment, or something else. It will be apparent once you get started where next to focus. The *Team Member Prosperity and Success Model* will always be a work in progress, needing continuous refinement as you learn to enable economically fragile people to give their best and thrive in your company.

Some Closing Thoughts

We have shared with you our mission, our culture—The Dasher Way—and our model for prosperity and success. We have offered examples drawn from our experience and lessons learned along the way.

As we conclude, here are a few ideas we hope readers will take away from our book.

As Seth Godin writes in his blog, our work may not be what we think it is.[35] It may be much bigger than we perceive. In other words, there is a much bigger picture than viewing our job as delivering services and being paid—we can view it as our job to bring good into the world.

The projects that we work on are going to be forgotten. The company we are building will probably one day be forgotten. The things we accomplish, the awards we receive, all this fades. What lasts is the influence that we have on people and the ways that we impact their lives for the better. And if we do it right, we can impact not just one generation but multiple generations.

The Dasher Challenge

What is the Dasher Challenge? That challenge is to take the ideas that we have shared here and apply them. We believe the time is ripe for this to become a movement in the business community to support low-wage, economically fragile workers to be successful in their lives and in their careers.

A movement happens when people gather around a single idea or call and then do something about it. We invite everyone to join our movement to improve the lives of low-wage, economically fragile workers.

There is a business case for doing this. We have talked a lot about that business case in terms of being able to tap into a pool of talent at a time when it is extremely hard to find workers.

Becoming part of this movement can help businesses to differentiate themselves in a way other than just trying to have the lowest price or best quality or most awesome service or some other universal claim. Doing something that brings good into our world is a differentiating factor which people everywhere can embrace and want to be part of.

Consider taking the Lead with Purpose Leaders' Pledge created by John Dame, author, strategist and leadership coach. (www. johndame.com)[36] John says, "As a young man, I always looked for an authentic reason to go to work. Today, for me, purpose has become a wide-open campaign to transform the workplace."

LEAD WITH PURPOSE LEADERS' PLEDGE

I commit to being a *Lead with Purpose Leader.*

1. **I stay** connected to my unique and true calling so that I am not afraid to fully live to that calling.

2. **I value** people more than money and things. If I prioritize people in my organization, profits take care of themselves.

3. **I ensure** the financial viability of my company so that we will make money and do good.

4. **I will cultivate** a culture where each person has opportunities

to learn, grow, and do their best.

5. **I win** by making sure there are no losers. When facing decisions, I will always insist on the right choice.

6. **I choose** calm over chaos. My employees thrive when they can connect and communicate.

7. **I explore and understand** my biases. Requesting, hearing, and valuing input is essential.

8. **I will lead** with compassion. Compassion drives belief and hope.

9. **I will be** curious and slow to judgment. I must be a well-informed decision maker.

10. **I will reconnect** with the *Lead with Purpose Leadership Pledge* daily. This routine will help me develop as a *Purposeful Leader.*[37]

In the end, all we can say is, try it. Try this in your own business, or if somehow the nature of your business does not accommodate doing this, then work with companies like Dasher. You will still be supporting the movement by allowing these companies to serve more people.

Thank you so much for reading.

If you want to keep up on what Dasher is doing, follow us on Facebook or LinkedIn. Visit our website at www.dasherinc.com.

Notes

[1] "Usual Weekly Earnings of Wage and Salary Workers Fourth Quarter 2018," Bureau of Labor Statistics, https://www.bls.gov/news.release/pdf/wkyeng.pdf, accessed Apr. 12, 2019.

[2] "Job Openings and Labor Turnover Summary February 2019," Bureau of Labor Statistics, https://www.bls.gov/news.release/jolts.nro.htm, accessed Apr. 12, 2019.

[3] Stephen Diorio, "The Financial Power of Brand Preference," *Forbes Magazine*, January 2019, https://www.forbes.com/sites/forbesinsights/2019/01/22/the-financial-power-of-brand-preference/#264f5686701b, accessed Apr. 12, 2019.

[4] "Driving corporate growth through social Impact: Four corporate archetypes to maximize your social impact," Deloitte, https://www2.deloitte.com/content/dam/Deloitte/us/Documents/strategy/us-strategy-operations-social-impact-corporate-archetypes.pdf, accessed Apr. 12, 2019.

[5] Gloria Guzman, Kirby G. Posey, Alemayehu Bishaw and Craig Benson, "Poverty Rates Higher, Median Household Income Lower in Rural Counties Than in Urban Areas," United States Census Bureau, December 6, 2018, https://www.census.gov/library/stories/2018/12/differences-in-income-growth-across-united-states-counties.html, accessed Feb. 22, 2019.

[6] News Release, "Five-Year Trends Available for Median Household Income, Poverty Rates and Computer and Internet Use," December 6, 2019, United States Census Bureau, https://www.census.gov/newsroom/press-releases/2018/2013-2017-acs-5year.html, accessed Feb. 22, 2019.

[7] American Community Survey, United States Census Bureau, https://www.census.gov/acs/www/data/data-tables-and-tools/data-profiles/2017/, accessed Feb. 22, 2019.

[8] "Survey of Income and Program Participation," United States Census Bureau, https://www.census.gov/sipp, accessed Feb. 22, 2019.

[9] "Living Wage Calculation for Dauphin County, Pennsylvania," http://livingwage.mit.edu/counties/42043, accessed Feb. 23, 2019.

[10] Michael J. R. Martin, "For the First Time, Census Bureau Data Show Impact of Geography, Income on Broadband Internet Access," December 6, 2018, United States Census Bureau, https://www.census.gov/library/stories/2018/12/rural-and-lower-income-counties-lag-nation-internet-subscription.html, accessed Feb. 23, 2019.

[11] Teresa Miller, quoted in "From blueprint to action: Working to end hunger in Pennsylvania," *The Impact*, Pennsylvania Department of Human Services, October 31, 2018.

[12] "Pennsylvania Fair Market Rent for 2019," https://www.rentdata.org/states/pennsylvania/2019, accessed Feb. 23, 2019.

[13] Build Healthy Places Network, https://www.buildhealthyplaces.org/about-us/, accessed Feb. 23, 2019.

[14] Rachel Garfield, Robin Rudowitz, and Anthony Damico, "Understanding the Intersection of Medicaid and Work," Henry J. Kaiser Family Foundation, (January 5, 2018), https://www.kff.org/medicaid/issue-brief/understanding-the-intersection-of-medicaid-and-work/, accessed Feb. 23, 2019.

[15] Leila Janah, *Give Work: Reversing Poverty One Job at a Time* (New York: Portfolio/Penguin, 2017), 68.

[16] "Social Determinants of Health," World Health Organization, https://www.who.int/social_determinants/sdh_definition/en/, accessed Feb. 23, 2019.

[17] "Meet ALICE," United Way of Northern New Jersey, http://www.unitedwaynnj.org/ourwork/alice.php, accessed Feb. 23, 2019.

[18] Seth Godin, *Tribes: We Need You to Lead Us*, (New York: Portfolio/Penguin, 2008), 1.

[19] Ritz Carlton, http://www.ritzcarlton.com/en/about/gold-standards, accessed Apr. 17, 2019.

[20] Dave Ramsey, Foreword to Chris Hogan, *Retire Inspired: It's Not an Age, It's a Financial Number,* (Brentwood, TN: Ramsey Press, 2016).

[21] David Friedman, *Fundamentally Different,* (West Conshohocken, PA: Infinity Publishing, 2014), 35.

[22] Tom Foster, *Hiring Talent: Decoding Levels of Work in the Behavioral Interview,* (Foster Learning, 2013), 87.

[23] SmartDollar, https://www.smartdollar.com/.

[24] Quentin Fottrell, "Most Americans have less than $1,000 in Savings," https://www.marketwatch.com/story/most-americans-have-less-than-1000-in-savings-2015-10-06, accessed Feb. 25, 2019.

[25] Benjamin Snyder, "About Half of U.S. Families Would Have a Tough Time With a Surprise $400 Expense," *Fortune*, http://fortune.com/2016/05/26/400-dollar-expense-study/, accessed Feb. 25, 2019.

[26] Entrepreneurial Operating System®, https://www.eosworldwide.com/, accessed Feb. 25, 2019.

[27] The John Maxwell Company, "7 Factors That Influence Influence," July 8, 2013, https://www.johnmaxwell.com/blog/7-factors-that-influence-influence/, accessed Feb. 25, 2019.

[28] Vincent J. Felitti et al., "Relationship of Childhood Abuse and Household Dysfunction to Many of the Leading Causes of Death in Adults," American Journal of Preventive Medicine, Vol. 14, No. 4, May 1998, https://www.ajpmonline.org/article/S0749-3797(98)00017-8/pdf.

[29] "State of the American Workplace," Gallup, https://news.gallup.com/reports/178514/state-american-workplace.aspx?g_source=ServiceLandingPage&g_medium=copy&g_campaign=tabs, accessed Apr. 12, 2019.

[30] Sean Gregory, "Serena Williams Opens Up About Her Complicated

Comeback, Motherhood And Making Time to Be Selfish," *Time*, August 16, 2018, http://time.com/5368858/serena-williams-comeback, accessed Feb. 25, 2019.

[31] "Adverse Childhood Experiences (ACES)," Centers for Disease Control and Prevention, https://www.cdc.gov/violenceprevention/childabuseandneglect/acestudy/index.html?CDC_AA_refVal=https%3A%2F%2Fwww.cdc.gov%2Fviolenceprevention%2Facestudy%2Findex.html, accessed Feb. 25, 2019.

[32] Karin Martinson and Pamela A. Holcomb, Urban Institute Research Report, "Innovative Employment Approaches and Programs for Low-Income Families," May 17, 2007, https://www.urban.org/research/publication/innovative-employment-approaches-and-programs-low-income-families, accessed Feb. 25, 2019.

[33] Carol Dweck, *Mindset: The New Psychology of Success*, (New York: Ballantine Books, 2006), 10.

[34] Matthew Kelly, *The Dream Manager*, (New York: Beacon Publishing, 2007), 4.

[35] Seth Godin, "But are you doing your work?", July 9, 2018, https://seths.blog/2018/07/but-are-you-doing-your-job, accessed Feb. 25, 2019.

[36] http://www.johndame.com/, accessed Feb. 25, 2019.

[37] "Leadership Pledge," https://www.johndame.com, accessed Mar. 13, 2019.

About the Authors

Sharon acquired Dasher, Inc., in 2009 with the goal of creating a forward-thinking and community-focused business that helps people to live happy healthy lives. To do this, she transformed Dasher from a shipping and mailing production line environment to a data-driven, customer contact, services operation.

Sharon Ryan, MBA
Chief Executive Officer

Sharon has a long service record supporting both commerce and the community of central Pennsylvania. She chaired the Capital Region Economic Development Corporation (CREDC) in 2015, having led the 2013 CREDC Campaign and raised $2.5 million. Sharon also chaired the United Way of the Capital Region's Annual Campaign in 2013, successfully raising $12 million to meet the needs of the less fortunate. She currently serves on the PennHOSA Foundation board, an organization dedicated to providing scholarships for higher education in health service professions.

Sharon is a graduate of Shippensburg University, earned an MBA from William Howard Taft University, is a long-time member of Vistage International, and holds Pennsylvania insurance agent licenses for life, health, annuities, property, and casualty.

As Dasher's executive in charge of our culture and engagement, Cynthia draws upon her extensive experience as a people leader of large organizations. An insurance industry executive, she developed expertise as well in business management, strategy development, process optimization, and performance measurement. Her nonprofit leadership gained Cynthia expertise in grant making and law enforcement.

Cynthia Tolsma
MBA, CPCU, CLU,
Chief Culture and
Engagement Officer

Before joining Dasher, Cynthia oversaw eight regional operations totaling $7 billion in revenue for Nationwide Insurance as field operations vice president. As executive director of an anti-crime authority, she led Pennsylvania's successful effort to reduce auto theft through grant making, law enforcement training, and public awareness.

Cynthia has chaired the United Way of the Capital Region Board of Directors and has held board and committee leadership positions for UPMC Pinnacle Health System, Pinnacle Health Medical Group, the United Way Foundation, and the Foundation for Enhancing Communities. She has served on the board and as a program volunteer with the Brethren Housing Association, which rehabilitates apartments for homeless single women with children and helps them build a future.

A graduate of Swarthmore College, Cynthia earned an MBA from the University of North Carolina at Chapel Hill, along with Certified Property-Casualty Underwriter and Certified Life Underwriter designations.

www.ExpertPress.net